Mafia and
Organized Crime
A Beginner's Guide

From anarchism to artificial intelligence and genetics to global terrorism, **BEGINNERS GUIDES** equip readers with the tools to fully understand the most challenging and important debates of our age. Written by experts in a clear and accessible style, books in this series are substantial enough to be thorough but compact enough to be read by anyone wanting to know more about the world they live in.

anarchism
ruth kinna

anti-capitalism
simon tormey

artificial intelligence
blay whitby

biodiversity
john spicer

bioterror & biowarfare
malcolm dando

the brain
a. al-chalabi, m. r. turner
& r. s. delamont

christianity
keith ward

cloning
aaron d. levine

criminal psychology
ray bull *et al.*

democracy
david beetham

energy
vaclav smil

evolution
burton s. guttman

evolutionary psychology
r. dunbar, l.barrett &
j. lycett

fair trade
jacqueline decarlo

genetics
a. griffiths, b.guttman,
d. suzuki & t. cullis

global terrorism
leonard weinberg

hinduism
klaus k. klostermaier

life in the universe
lewis dartnell

mafia & organized crime
james o. finckenauer

NATO
jennifer medcalf

the palestine–israeli conflict
dan cohn-sherbok &
dawoud el-alami

philosophy of mind
edward feser

postmodernism
kevin hart

quantum physics
alastair i. m. rae

religion
martin forward

the small arms trade
m. schroeder, r. stohl
& d. smith

FORTHCOMING:

animal behaviour

beat generation

bioethics

british politics

censorship

climate change

conspiracy theories

crimes against humanity

engineering

ethics

existentialism

extrasolar planets

feminist theory

forensic science

galaxies

gender & sexuality

globalization

history of science

human rights

humanism

immigration

indigenous peoples

literary theory

modern slavery

oil

philosophy of religion

political philosophy

racism

radical philosophy

renaissance art

romanticism

socialism

time

volcanoes

Mafia and Organized Crime
A Beginner's Guide

James O. Finckenauer

ONEWORLD

OXFORD

MAFIA AND ORGANIZED CRIME

A Oneworld Book
Published by Oneworld Publications 2007

ISBN-13: 978–1–85168–526–4

Typeset by Jayvee, Trivandrum, India
Cover design by Two Associates
Printed and bound by TJ International Ltd.,
Padstow, Cornwall

Oneworld Publications
185 Banbury Road
Oxford OX2 7AR
England
www.oneworld-publications.com

Learn more about Oneworld. Join our mailing list to
find out about our latest titles and special offers at:

www.oneworld-publications.com

Contents

Foreword

"As above, so below" was one of the central tenets of the ancient hermetic philosophies – the world in which humans lived was a reflection of the glories of Heaven, but at the same time, the heavens were affected by what happened on the mortal Earth. What connection does this have to organized crime? The underworld is shaped by the "upperworld" but also shapes it. The decision of the US government to introduce Prohibition reshaped the North American underworld, while the collapse of the Soviet Union unleashed a new form of organized crime on the world. There can be little doubt that organized crime and its pernicious activities has a direct impact on the modern world, whether in facilitating the activities of international terrorists or in polluting the global money supply with "dirty" funds.

When societies get organized, so too do their criminals, and organized crime has evolved as the shadowy underside of modernization and order. A dark, common, thread runs through human history, from the smugglers and protection racketeers of ancient Rome, to the surprisingly sophisticated economic substructures which supported and flourished on the back of seventeenth-century piracy, to today's cybercriminals and a global drug trade worth an estimated $500 billion a year. Organized crime exists because it supplies needs not satisfied by the legitimate sector, such as narcotics and vice, or inadequately controlled by the state, such as protection rackets. However, it is at its most dangerous when it doesn't just exploit the weaknesses of the state, but it begins to replace it.

Jim Finckenauer usefully draws a distinction between organized crime and mafias. The former is essentially a description of an activity, but the latter is a culture of criminality, a sub-set of organized crime that embeds itself in society by filling needs that in more ideal circumstances would be the preserve of the state. What does it say about the experience of migration to the United States that so many communities, as they arrived, created their own forms of organized crime, from the Irish and Jewish gangs of the nineteenth century to the *Cosa Nostra* of the Italians? Feeling locked out of the opportunities for which they had made the long and hazardous journey to the New World, the migrants felt disenfranchised, and neglected. In their violent and parasitic way, the gangs offered a sense of identity and opportunity, and social mobility. Why were the *yakuza* crime gangs of Japan only criminalized in the 1990s, before which they were openly accepted and even respected? To a large extent because the *yakuza* were considered "reliable," because it was felt that organized crime could be used to control "disorganized crime" and at the same time buttress the power of the existing political and economic elite. Understanding mafias and organized crime helps us understand the wider world in which they operate.

To this end, this useful primer to the phenomenon quite rightly starts with a simple question that begs a complex answer: what is organized crime? Sometimes, the mobsters are easy to identify, a collection of ne'er-do-wells with no visible source of income but owning flashy cars and homes; involved in the staples of organized criminality, whether trafficking drugs or infiltrating legitimate businesses. The old stereotypes, which were always something of a caricature, are becoming even less applicable in the modern world. Today's "OC" could as easily be an apparently legitimate businessperson whose portfolio of interests ranges from the entirely "clean" through to overtly criminal, or who facilitates the activities of more conventional criminals. Or they might be a fringe member of a radical movement, involved in raising funds for political or terrorist operations through crime, but doing so less out of a belief in the cause than for the generous proportion of its income they pocket. In some cases, not only do political leaders engage in organized crime, but local and national governments almost become gangs in their own right, whether for personal enrichment or – as in North Korea – to raise funds for a bankrupt state. Failing that, gangs may be powerful enough to create their own "states-within-states," from the poppy fields of Afghanistan to Morocco's cannabis-growing Rif region.

Global crime is not an organized global conspiracy, but nor is it a random collection of maladjusted thugs, frauds, and psychopaths. It is a complex array of competing, cooperating, stable, fragmenting, local, and multinational organizations. It is powerful, growing, and above all, transnational, something on which Finckenauer has a distinctive perspective, thanks to his experience not only as an academic social scientist but also the former head of the National Institute of Justice's International Center. Modern consumers take it for granted that they can buy food from halfway round the world, fly north for skiing and south for the sun, and talk with their friends on their cellphones while traveling to work. These explosions in communications, mobility, and global economic interconnectivity have also revolutionized the underworld. What happens around the globe affects all our lives.

Finckenauer helpfully takes the focus away from individual groups and underworld cultures, whether Italian American wiseguys or tattooed *Yakuza*, and looks at the businesses at the heart of modern organized crime. So long as there is a demand for illegal narcotics, so long as people want to find new lives for themselves regardless of immigration quotas, and so long as there are societies in which people cannot or will not rely on their legitimate governments, then mafias and organized crime will find a market. Criminals are often good businesspeople, and quickly adapt to new pressures and opportunities. The Latin American *narcotraficantes* trade some of their cocaine for heroin from

Figure 2 The Hells Angels outlaw motorcycle gang has some 85 chapters in 15 countries. Their criminal enterprises include prostitution, illegal pornography, extortion, fraudulent telemarketing, and drug trafficking.

European gangs to diversify their stock, like any modern entrepreneur. Hells Angels (and other outlaw motorcycle 'gangs') and Vietnamese groups use modern hydroponic techniques (in which plants are grown indoors in nutrient solutions rather than in soil) to make Canada a net exporter of marijuana.

Organized crime is the dark side of organized society. The police and courts can break up specific gangs, prosecute individual criminals, and make life harder for mobsters. However, the best we can hope for is to minimize the impact of organized crime, to keep it at the fringes of the legitimate economy, and prevent it from penetrating, subverting or destabilizing democratic societies. While, for understandable reasons, the eyes of the world's security forces are presently focused on fighting terrorism, more people die and more lives are ruined every year from mob-related violence, from narcotics, and from the systematic exploitation of vulnerable women and children than al-Qaeda could ever dream of.

Finckenauer is right to devote particular attention to the growing phenomenon of people-trafficking. Illegal migration and the trafficking of humans for sexual and other purposes are not just global tragedies, they are also challenges to transnational security, not least in the way they undermine the integrity of national borders, and encourage other activities, such as drug smuggling. The link between crime and security is present in many of the activities of organized crime. Thriving markets in illegal firearms, fake identities, and documents and money laundering services help terrorism immeasurably. Criminality can penetrate, and even subvert, national military and security structures. In Russia, military aircraft (which are not subject to customs checks) fly drugs from the Afghan border into Moscow, Spetsnaz commandoes moonlight as mob hitmen, and military vehicles have been written off as destroyed and then are sold on to criminals for resale, including two helicopters which reportedly ended up in the hands of the Colombian Cali drug cartel.

As above, so below. Organized crime is not just a threat to states and global institutions, but also has an impact, sometimes obvious, sometimes indirect, on the lives of almost every citizen of the world. Even in the best-policed, most stable and secure cities and countries, mob-trafficked narcotics breed petty crime (driving up insurance rates and creating a climate of insecurity), organized crime gangs commit identity theft and fraud, and the operations of corrupt cartels and protection racketeers jack up the prices charged to customers. This is as nothing to the overt mayhem visited on those living in the heartlands of organized crime – from the poor *barrios* of Latin America to the crumbling slums of Palermo – but emphasizes that no one is immune from the effects of organized crime.

As Finckenauer so rightly concludes, managing organized crime and minimizing its capacity to harm society depends not just on the apparatus of the state, from the police and courts to the lawmakers, but also on mobilizing people against its threat. Whether this is in creating a public demand for tough action (as helped galvanize the fight against the Sicilian Mafia after the murder of the well-respected magistrates Giovanni Falcone and Paolo Borsellino in 1992), refusing the goods and services organized crime peddles, or breaking the old habit of *omerta* (silence). Mafias thrive in the gulf between state and society, and by bringing the two together, the mobsters can be cut down to size.

Mark Galeotti

1

Organized crime and the Mafia *

Organized crime is both more and less than the average person understands it to be. It is more pervasive, more dangerous, and more diverse; a worldwide problem, closely linked to concerns about global terrorism and much more than the *mafia* of the popular media. It is less romantic, much less "what I don't know won't hurt me" in its impact, and a lot less "Italian" in its appearance. Perhaps most surprisingly, to a considerable degree it owes its existence to people who consider they are upstanding, law-abiding citizens. In the words Walt Kelly put into the mouth of his cartoon character Pogo: "We have met the enemy, and he is us!" So it is with much of organized crime.

In the beginning

Clodius, an extraordinary character, was perhaps the world's very first "godfather" of organized crime; he flourished during the decade 59–50 BCE in ancient Rome. Said to be without any redeeming characteristics, he led a Roman mob for five years. Clodius:

> ... defied justice, insulted the Consuls, beat the Tribunes, paraded the streets with a gang of armed slaves, killing persons disagreeable

* A slightly different version of this discussion appeared in *Trends in Organized Crime*, Vol. 8, No. 3, Spring 2005. Copyright permission granted by Transaction Publishers.

to him; and in the Senate itself he had high friends and connections, who threw a shield over him when his audacity had gone
beyond endurance.

http//ancienthistory.about.com/library/bl/bl_
pennellhistoryofrome31.htm

Clodius's chief rival was another disreputable character and
godfather-like figure, Milo. Milo's fame was gained in the schools
of the gladiators. Gangs of armed slaves accompanied him everywhere, and there were constant collisions between his gang and
Clodius's. A long struggle between these two ruffians ended with
Milo murdering Clodius. Milo was impeached for this crime (he
held public office at the time) and sent into exile at Massilia. Thus
ended one of the earliest-known gang wars.

Jumping ahead more than a thousand years, to the sixteenth
century, we find more evidence of the long history of organized
crime. For about three hundred years, from about 1500, the world
suffered through the "golden age of piracy." Piracy was a form of
organized crime, involving hijacking, theft, black marketeering,
corruption and political connections. Although piracy had certainly existed before the "golden age," among the Phoenicians,
Greeks and Romans, this was its heyday. Men like Henry
Morgan, Blackbeard, Captain Kidd, and Black Bart led pirate
ships and their crews of thugs in plunder – and any ship carrying
goods was fair game.

The pirate bands exemplify many of the characteristics that we
have come to associate with professional criminal organizations of
more recent vintage: hierarchical structures and systematic use of
violence and corruption. Piracy is by no means extinct; it thrives
today, especially in Southeast Asia and the Caribbean.

The above examples should belie any preconceived notion that
organized crime is a modern phenomenon. On the contrary, corruption, racketeering, bribery, violence, extortion, intimidation,
and loan-sharking stretch back into classical antiquity. Let us

step back and try to make clear exactly what we mean by "organized crime."

The problem of definition

In my experience, talking about organized crime with almost anyone quickly establishes that they have some view of what organized crime is: it is neither an obscure nor an esoteric topic. But what is the prevailing view? My sources are mostly American, although I have had similar conversations with Russians, Chinese, Germans, Canadians, Mexicans, and others.

The predominant view among Americans fits the stereotype that organized crime is synonymous with what they conceive of as the Italian "mafia," meaning the Italian mafia in the United States, also known as *La Cosa Nostra*. Occasionally, they refer to the "real" Italian mafia in Italy (especially Sicily), the so-called Russian "mafia," Chinese gangs or triads, or Colombian and Mexican drug traffickers. Corporate criminals, and groups such as the Irish Republican Army, are sometimes mentioned.

The main sources of information are the popular media – television, movies, newspapers, and magazines. Some have seen the movies in *The Godfather* series, or *Goodfellas*, or more recent films. The American television show *The Sopranos* is especially influential. News coverage shapes the views of some people but only rarely does anyone have first-hand information. And almost as rare is someone who has read a book – usually a novel – about organized crime.

I suspect this picture is neither unusual nor unique to my particular contacts. It is probably true of the vast majority of the American public, and, given the powerful presence of American media in other countries, of a wider public. It is safe to say that almost everyone knows something about, and has an opinion about, organized crime. I see my task not as writing on a blank slate but as trying to erase and correct some of what is already written. I want to inform, but especially to challenge, existing opinions and question the predominant stereotypes of organized crime.

In its 1986 report, the US President's Commission on Organized Crime indicated that the problem of defining organized crime lay not in the word *crime*, but in the word *organized*. This reflected the conclusion reached by the Swedish criminologist, Thorsten Sellin, nearly fifty years before. Acts such as murder, robbery, and theft – said to be *mala in se*, or wrong in and of themselves – are well defined and accepted as crimes. Other acts, such as prostitution, drug dealing, bribery, and gambling – labeled *mala prohibita*, or wrong because they are prohibited – while less clearly defined, are also generally accepted as crimes. All these acts, as well as hijacking, extortion, loan-sharking, bootlegging, fixing sports events, and smuggling, have come to be associated with what is commonly thought of as "organized crime."

However, a list does not define organized crime, because these offenses can also be committed by criminals acting alone, or by criminals acting in groups that would not be regarded as being criminal "organizations." I will make this latter distinction clearer as we go along. The phenomenon of organized crime cannot be defined by its crimes alone: any definition must address, and account for, the elusive modifying term "organized."

Background

Two of the more informative syntheses of earlier work on the characteristics of criminal organizations in the United States were made by Frank Hagan (1983) and Michael Maltz (1985, 1994). Several caveats should apply to their efforts, although I do not mean their discussion is not useful, but that we should be mindful of their limits and not give them more credence than they are due. First, their sources have a definite US bias, both in terms of what is being described, and of who is describing it, secondly, many of those sources are rather dated, and third, within the overall focus, there is an additional limit arising from a further focus on a particular brand of American organized crime: *La Cosa Nostra* (LCN). Bearing these points in mind, their work still provides a helpful analytical framework.

Hagan identified eleven dimensions of organized crime. Maltz suggested nine; some identical to Hagan's and others that overlap. I have partially integrated these two approaches and offer the following list as a framework for beginning to think about what organized crime is and what criminal organizations are:

- ideology (or lack of)
- structure/organized hierarchy
- continuity
- violence/use of force or the threat of force
- restricted membership/bonding
- illegal enterprises
- penetration of legitimate businesses
- corruption

Years of research on organized crime in the United States indicated that organized crime groups were *non-ideological*: they did not have their own political agenda. In today's context, organized crime groups are different from terrorist organizations dedicated to political change. They do not espouse a particular political or religious ideology. Their interest in government is mostly in its nullification, through bribery, pay-offs, and corruption. According to the earlier view, terrorist organizations such as al-Qaeda would not be classified as a form of organized crime, despite the fact that they may engage in killings, bombings, and kidnappings, and crimes such as drug trafficking and gun-running. Maltz, in his later work (1994), recognized that this particular distinction has become blurred. Criminal organizations may collaborate with terrorist organizations, and terrorist groups may engage in crimes, especially drug trafficking, to finance their activities.

The blurring between ideological and non-ideological is very much evident in this comment from the US National Academy of Sciences:

> [T]errorism may be importantly connected to other kinds of transnational crime, either because some criminal groups are enlisted in terrorist acts, or terrorists themselves act for pecuniary as well as political motives, or because some terrorist groups use criminal means to achieve their non-monetary aims
>
> National Research Council, 1999:6

There was also fairly widespread agreement that organized crime groups had a *well-structured hierarchy*, with leaders or bosses, and followers in descending order of authority. Followers included associates, hangers-on, and would-be members (often referred to as "wannabes"). Within this structure, members of the group conspire to commit crimes but the group has someone who decides what will be done, by whom, how, and when. Today, this sort of organization is still found in some criminal groups: for example, the outlaw motorcycle gangs that I will describe later. These gangs, or chapters, generally have a president, vice president, secretary, treasurer, and even a sergeant at arms, elected by the membership, but they are the exception rather than the rule. More common are the loosely-affiliated networks of criminals, who coalesce around specific criminal opportunities. The structure of these groups is much more amorphous and free-floating, with a flatter, less-rigid hierarchy.

Continuity means that the group is self-perpetuating; continuing beyond the life or participation of any particular individual. Bosses who die, or go to jail, are replaced by new bosses. Others may drop out, for various reasons, but the organization – like its counterparts in the non-criminal world – continues. Maltz (1994) suggests that a criminal group's involvement in continuing enter-prises (drug distribution, extortion, or gambling) – what he means by *continuity* – is one of the cohesive elements of a "true" orga-nized crime group. This continuity is maintained over time and across crimes, and remains an important definitional element of what is truly organized crime.

Violence and the threat of violence are also very much generally accepted as important dimensions of organized crime. Organized criminal groups use force, or threaten its use, to accomplish their ends. They engage in killings, beatings, burnings, and destruction. Violence is used against other criminals and against victims who do not pay for their drugs, pay off their bets or pay back their loans, and is used to frighten and intimidate extortion victims and poten-tial competitors.

Criminal organizations generally *restrict membership* according to certain criteria: for example, ethnicity, kinship, race, or criminal background. Membership of LCN, Chinese gangs, and the Japanese *Yakuza* is based on ethnicity; in the former Soviet Union, the *vory v zakone* (thieves–in–law) were formed in the prison camps of the Soviet Gulag. These professional criminals thus share a common background and common circumstances. Membership of criminal organizations such as the Aryan Brotherhood or the Black Guerilla Family depends on both racial and criminal consid-erations. The exclusivity characteristic of some criminal organiza-tions might also include bonding rituals such as initiations, the wearing of colors, tattoos, the use of signs, and so on, defining characteristics of street gangs.

It is widely agreed that organized crime exists for economic gain. Making a profit, by whatever means necessary, is a primary goal of organized criminal groups. This partly why they are believed to be non-ideological, and thus different from terrorist organizations. Profit can come from *illegal enterprises* such as drugs, gambling, or loan-sharking, or from legal businesses. For example, investing in restaurants or bars both accords respectable social status and is a good way to launder illegal money. Money laundering is a method of accounting for money obtained through illegal means: for example, money obtained through extortion can be recorded, for tax purposes, as having come from a bar. Maltz (1994) indicates that there are many good reasons for organized crime groups to diversify into *legitimate businesses*, but that does not mean that all of them do. This may be especially seen when we examine transnational organized crime and/or organized crime in different countries.

Organized crime exists to provide goods and services that are illegal, regulated, or in short supply. The presence of one or more of these limiting conditions, and the desire (by a large enough segment of society) for those particular goods or services, makes their provision a profitable business. Many people want drugs, sex, or to be able to gamble; some want to dispose of toxic wastes cheaply and quickly; others want to obtain illegal weapons, adopt babies without having to go through a lot of bureaucratic red tape, or collect on life insurance policies prematurely. The tug-of-war between human desires and human weaknesses, and laws, regulations, and morals provides fat profits for organized crime.

Organized crime generally seeks to neutralize or nullify government by avoiding investigation, arrest, prosecution, and convictions, through pay-offs to police, prosecutors, or legal officials. *Corruption* of public officials and the political process is very characteristic of organized crime, but may not be employed by every criminal group (See Maltz, 1994:27). Pay-offs enable organized crime groups to operate with immunity. Bribery of purchasing agents, union officials, politicians, and others facilitates organized crime's infiltration of legitimate businesses. The huge profits, and the temptations and inducements that can be offered to relatively lowly-paid public servants, undermine the efforts of law enforcement agencies to combat organized crime. Even high-level officials and political figures are subject to corruption, particularly in developing countries, and countries that have suffered economic collapse and civil and military strife.

Evidence that elements of this framework for looking at organized crime are both still viable and applicable to the analysis of organized crime around the world, is seen in a recent description of organized crime in China. He Bingsong describes what he called "underground criminal groups" as having "an established leader," "core members," a "distinctly layered hierarchy," and a "set of procedures or an initiation ceremony for joining the organization" (Bingsong, 2003:282).

We should keep these dimensions in mind as we explore and examine organized crime in both its national and transnational forms.

Why is definition important?

While my premise is that definition is important, I recognize that, in the case of organized crime, it has been controversial. The public's perception of organized crime, and how seriously they regard it, determines the degree of support for policies and resources to combat it. How organized crime is defined goes a long way toward determining how laws are framed, how investigations and prosecutions are conducted, how research is carried out, and, increasingly, how mutual legal assistance across national borders is (or is not) rendered. Existing substantial differences in opinions and views of what exactly is "organized crime," make these practices, from law enforcement to research, more complicated.

An example of the difficulty of defining organized crime is found in the work of the United Nations *Convention on Transnational Organized Crime*, from the late 1990s. Agreement on a definition proved to be the most difficult issue for the negotiators, and they ended up with a very broad, lowest-common-denominator definition, which I shall discuss shortly.

Legal definitions in criminal statutes – both in the United States and elsewhere – have been either non-existent, constitutionally vague or indefinite, or overly broad. Various US government commissions and investigative bodies – and organizations in many other countries – have markedly differed in their definitions, and in some cases have failed to define the phenomenon at all. The relatively few academic criminologists who have studied and written on this topic also differ dramatically in their conceptualizations.

According to the law

Since crime is defined by law, the legal definitions of organized crime may be the most important issue. Definitions contained in criminal or civil statutes target specific acts as being legally proscribed and sharply and narrowly define what behavior is subject to criminal or civil remedy. In the United States, criminals, whether organized or not, cannot be prosecuted and punished simply because they have certain characteristics or belong to certain groups. They can only be prosecuted and punished if they have committed illegal acts. While it may be that, in the words of the old adage, "if it looks like a duck, walks like a duck, and hangs around with ducks, then it is a duck," no one – in the US – can be prosecuted just for looking like, walking like, or hanging around with members of organized crime groups. (This principle does not apply everywhere. In Italy, being a member of the mafia is, in itself, a crime. Membership of a "Mafia-type" association, defined as one in which "members systematically use intimidation and conditions of subjection deriving therefrom to commit crimes, to gain control over economic activities and to acquire unlawful advantages" (Adamoli, et al., 1998:6) is a criminal offense.) In the 2000 United Nations *Convention Against Transnational Crime*, participation in organized criminal groups is classified as a criminal act.) Even in the US, as shown by the Racketeer

Influenced and Corrupt Organizations (RICO) Act of 1970, definitions can be unclear. G. Robert Blakey, father of RICO, posed the issue of legal definition quite baldly. At that time, he said there was "no generally applicable legal definition of concepts of 'organized crime,' 'corruption' or 'racket' or 'racketeering' " (President's Commission, 1986:511). The legal definitions, according to Blakey, were (and are) often constitutionally vague or indefinite, possibly violating constitutional rights to association and assembly, and concepts of due process or equal protection, or raising other civil liberties issues and problems. In any or all of these instances, criminal charges against suspected organized crime defendants can be dismissed or convictions overturned on appeal.

The only definition of organized crime contained in a US statute is that in Public Law 90–351, the Omnibus Crime Control and Safe Streets Act of 1968:

> Organized crime means the unlawful activities of the members of a highly organized, disciplined association engaged in supplying illegal goods and services, including but not limited to gambling, prostitution, loan sharking, narcotics, labor racketeering, and other unlawful activities of members of organizations.

This statement defines organized crime partly in terms of its organization, but more in terms of a list of crimes.

Difficulties can arise when and if this particular definition is used as the basis for bringing criminal charges. What, for example, constitutes a "highly organized, disciplined association" as opposed to one which is less highly-organized, or less-disciplined? The distinction is vital for separating defendants charged with organized crime from defendants who, as individuals, gamble, engage in prostitution, make loans for exorbitant interest rates, or sell drugs. Law enforcement can readily proceed against individuals charged with unlawful activities, but in many countries it is much less clear that it can proceed against individuals who are simply members of an organization, even when those organizations are suspected of being involved in unlawful activities.

Interestingly, but perhaps not surprisingly, given the difficulties involved, the US Organized Crime Control Act of 1970 (PL 91–452) did not define organized crime. Particular provisions of this act, especially the RICO statute, have been subject to legal tests and reviews to determine the constitutionality of their legal definitions. The reason why proceeding against an individual or individuals for being members of a criminal organization is not so clearly prohibited in US law is that RICO enables prosecutors to charge entire groups determined to be affiliated with a criminal enterprise, and engaged in a "pattern of racketeering activity." The matter of what ought to be public policy with respect to organized crime is related to the legal issue. An expert group commissioned by the Council of Europe defined the mandatory criteria for organized crime as: (1) collaboration of three or more people; (2) for a prolonged or indefinite period of time; (3) suspected or convicted of committing serious criminal offenses; and (4) having the objective of pursuing profit and/or power (*Conseil de l'Europe*, 1997).

Definition in the context of public policy is also important because it affects the allocation of financial and personnel resources for combating organized crime. Public policy making usually focuses on elements such as the nature of the problem, its magnitude, its seriousness, its rate of change over time, the people affected by it, geographical aspects, what responses have been attempted, projections of future scenarios, and what appear to be its sources or causes. Organized crime, where it exists, is clearly a public policy problem: how it is viewed, how big a problem it is perceived to be, how serious it is, if it is seen to be growing, who is being victimized by it, and whether it should be a priority, are bound to shape efforts to combat it. Specifically, the perceptions of the public and of public officials will influence resource allocation.

Building the knowledge base

Researchers and academics who attempt to understand and explain organized crime hope by doing so to support the policy-making process. Definition is therefore also very important in their work. The same is true of the journalists who study, and write about, organized crime. Journalists are particularly influential because they shape the views and opinions of the general public, and often of public officials. If we are to build a body of knowledge accumulated from a number of researchers and a variety of studies, common definition(s) will help insure consistency.

Many scholars, and journalists from many countries, have worked on this issue over the years. I will point to just a few. Donald R. Cressey served as a consultant to the 1967 US Presidential Commission Task Force on Organized Crime. Cressey focused on organized crime in the United States, equating it to a large extent with the Mafia or *La Cosa Nostra*. In his report, Cressey criticized the earlier efforts of social scientists to define organized crime, saying that they were unconcerned with the formal and informal structure and needed to attend to the anti-law attitudes that permit engagement in a "continuous" or "self-perpetuating" conspiracy. Organized criminals, said Cressey, exhibit certain attitudes towards the rules, agreements and understandings that form the foundation of the criminal social structure. This social structure and these attitudes differentiate organized crime and the organized criminal from other crimes and criminals.

Another consultant to the Commission, Thomas Schelling, concluded that monopoly and extortion were the unique defining characteristics of organized crime. According to Schelling (1971), organized crime seeks to gain exclusive control or influence over criminal markets, tolerating no competition, and using violence or threats of violence to drive out competitors. Under this definition, organized crime is most likely to be found in businesses that lend themselves to monopoly control.

Dwight Smith was one of those who criticized Cressey's definition of organized crime, saying it contributed to a "myth of the mafia," (a subject I will take up at length later). In his work, (for example, *The Mafia Mystique* (1975)), Smith's argument was that illicit enterprise could explain organized crime. His economic approach emphasized the activities (the criminal enterprise) over the individuals or group(s) undertaking the enterprise. Organized crime, he said, is different from legitimate organized business only because its activities fall at a different place in the spectrum of economic enterprise. Organized crime is essentially an economic operation whose business is to provide illegal goods and services.

Joseph Albini's ideas (1971) were similar to Smith's in many respects. Albini agreed that criminals involved in organized crime are illicit entrepreneurs. What he preferred to call "syndicated crime" consisted, he said, of loosely structured patron–client relationships in which roles, role expectations and benefits were a result of mutual agreement or obligation. Syndicated crime grows and thrives especially well in the United States, argued Albini, because Americans demand illicit goods and services behind a puritanical and suppressive façade. They are, in other words, hypocrites!

Francis Ianni and Elizabeth Ruess-Ianni likewise focused on US-based organized crime, and therefore defined it in terms of what they said was the unique character of American society:

> [W]e have defined organized crime as an integral part of the American social system that brings together (1) a public that demands certain goods and services that are defined as illegal, (2) an organization of individuals who produce or supply those goods and services, and (3) corrupt public officials who protect such individuals for their own profit or gain.
>
> (Ianni and Ruess-Ianni, 1976:xvi).

Of more recent students of organized crime, Peter Reuter defined it simply as the criminal activities of "gangs that have maintained a capacity for credible threats of violence over a long period of time" (Reuter, in Kelly, Chin, and Schatzberg, 1994:96). From this definition, a "reputation" that enhances both extortive and corruptive capacity, and the "durability" of that reputation are the essential characteristics for criminal organizations to be effective.

William Chambliss (1978, 1988) described what he called "state" organized crime, moving beyond the constraints of the unique character of American society and institutions to look more globally at what organized crime is, and what might be its common causes. Chambliss's theory was that criminal networks result from the responses of people in positions of power (including government officials) "to the contradictions that exist in the social structure of which they are a part" (Chambliss, 1988:208). These contradictions occur in every society – or at least every industrialized society – for example, between what is required and what is possible, what is wanted and what is available, and what is desired and what is legal. Organized crime, according to Chambliss, arises to help resolve these contradictions.

As organized crime has become much more global since the 1980s, and as the focus on transnational forms of organized crime sharpens, new scholars are adding to our knowledge and researching into organized crime elsewhere in the world. They include Ko-lin Chin (Chinese organized crime), Federico Varese (Russian organized crime), and Letizia Paoli (the Italian mafia), to name just a few. Klaus von Lampe, a German specialist, summed up the dilemma of definition for those attempting to study this particular form of crime:

> Organized crime is neither a clearly discernable empirical phenomenon, nor do we find an agreement on what its "essence" or "nature" might be. Rather, a broad range of people, structures and events are in varying degrees and combinations subsumed under this umbrella concept. Due to this elusiveness, the phrase "organized crime" was allowed to take on an existence of its own

quite independent from the social reality it supposedly relates to. Social scientists, then, not only face the challenge of nailing a "conceptual pudding" to the wall. They also have to deal with the duality of organized crime as a facet of social reality and as a social construct. In the latter capacity its associative and luring power strongly influences public perceptions, policy making and law enforcement towards a warlike attitude.

(von Lampe, in Duyne, von Lampe, and Passas, 2002:191).

The vagaries of definition – the conceptual pudding – allow stereotypes a strong foothold. The absence of solid rational-empirical evidence to refute them, the stereotypes themselves and the myths that surround them drive public perception, public policy, and law enforcement practices concerning organized crime. They also shape and constrain research and analysis.

Policies and practices grounded in myths and stereotypes are unlikely to succeed in the real world of criminal organizations and organized crime. Research that is biased by erroneous or preconceived notions is unlikely to be informative and enlightening. Perhaps one of the best examples of this are the myths and stereotypes that surround the term "mafia." I will return to the broader issue of the sometimes romantic notions and images of organized crime presented by the media, but first, I want to discuss the confusion caused by the conflation of "organized crime" and "mafia."

Organized crime and the mafia: same or different?

To many people, organized crime and the mafia are synonymous terms and concepts: a perception that is not only simplistic, but also incorrect. Furthermore, not only is it wrong to equate organized crime and mafia, but doing so has negative consequences for policy and practice.

There is certainly such a thing as *mafia*. It is neither a single entity, nor a single criminal group, nor even a collection of criminal groups. There are mafia associations that are indeed collections of criminal groups, but above and beyond these lies *mafia*, the social construct. *Mafia* is an idea; a cultural artifact that extends beyond the people, the places, and the activities that comprise it. A certain chemistry – an economic chemistry, a political chemistry, a cultural chemistry, or a historical chemistry – creates the fertile soil necessary for the growth of the mafia.

This fertile soil has existed for hundreds of years, but where is it found? First and foremost it is in the unique culture of Sicily. Some argue that southern Italy – home to the Calabrian *'Ndrangheta*, the Neapolitan *Camorra*, and the more recent *Sacra Corona Unita* – also qualify as being the origin of mafia associations. What is important is that, while the mafia is a unique and special form of criminal organization, it is not generic and all-encompassing. The mafia is very definitely a form of organized crime but, crucially, it is not the only form. Thus, the terms ought not be used interchangeably.

The well-known Italian legal scholar Adolfo Beria di Argentine described the mafia thus:

> The Mafia is a rural Mafia and an urban Mafia; it is a power of material control of territory and it is a power of exploitation of local and national administrative and political circuits and of intangible international financial circuits; it is a culture of *omerta*, taking refuge in the environment of underdevelopment and it is a culture of unscrupulousness in diverse and sophisticated international circuits; it is violence for profit and it is a structure of power which pervades all other powers.
>
> (Di Argentine, 1992:255).

In their recent book on the Sicilian Mafia, Schneider and Schneider (2003) describe Sicilian *mafiosi* as being "entrepreneurial, opportunistic, aggressive, [and] capable of violence" (p. 46). These characteristics describe many other criminals as well, both organized and unorganized. The Schneiders go on to explain how the mafiosi create local fraternities – the *cosche*. "Legitimated through a charter myth and ideology of honor, these mutual aid fraternities obligate their members to be 'silent before the law,' while supporting them through whatever brushes they may have with the police, the judiciary, and the prisons" (pp. 46–47).

These ideas of "men of honor," silence or *omerta*, supporting "made" members and their families when necessary, and especially of "wielding power through the systematic use of private violence" (Tilly, 1974:xiv) distinguish the mafia and mafia-like structures from other kinds of organized crime. The mafia focus on political power and sovereign control over their territory means, perhaps somewhat ironically, that the Sicilian mafia is not involved in many of the mainstream criminal activities generally associated with other criminal organizations. They hold a monopoly of the protection business, whereas other criminal organizations seek their monopolies in some illegal commodity, such as drugs, gambling or prostitution.

The history of the mafia in Sicily shows it developed as a socially embedded quasi-state. Mafiosi (or *gabelloti* (middlemen), as they were first known) acted as agents for absent landlords in "governing" Sicily at a time when formal government was either distant and alien or, at best, inefficient. Consequently, the mafia is unique in its strong exercise of a quasi-governmental role. Governments exercise their monopoly on violence through institutions such as the police and the military, which are legally granted the power to use force when necessary. But where governments are weak, or corrupt, or perhaps just terribly inefficient and ineffective, a power vacuum is created, which, like any vacuum, gets filled. The mafia, or mafia-like organizations, assume and develop power where and when the government cannot, or will not, exercise this monopoly. In certain societies, such as in

Sicily (and arguably now in places in the former Soviet Union, parts of Eastern Europe, and Africa) a mafia, or a mafia-type organization, has assumed responsibility for normally government functions such as contracting for public works, dispute resolution (via an informal court system), and especially, the provision of protection and security. Paoli describes the mafia in Sicily and Calabria as policing "the general population, settling conflicts, recovering stolen goods, and enforcing property rights laws ... [T]hey tax the main productive activities carried out within their territory ..." (Paoli, 2004).

Given that a mafia arises in a power vacuum, standing in place of the government in the use of violence, mafias are less likely to develop in strong stable democracies with robust institutions and a vibrant civil society. Countries such as Australia, Canada, Great Britain, France and the United States are good examples. They have vigorous democratic institutions (including effective police and military) and active civil societies thus, historically, the mafia has made few inroads into governance (an exception might be the domination by LCN, during much of the twentieth century, of large segments of the legitimate economy in New York City – see Jacobs, et al., 1999). Nonetheless, these countries still have their share of organized crime in a wide variety of forms. This, I believe, helps to support the argument that organized crime and the mafia are not the same.

Organized crime and criminal organizations

A simple list of crimes does not tell us much about organized crime. Crimes are committed by individuals either acting alone or in groups; groups that are one of the fundamental building blocks of organized crime. I prefer to think of these groups as social networks – networks that are often small, informal, and short-lived.

Obviously most networks are not criminal networks: everyone belongs to social networks (I hope not criminal ones) at work, school, church, or in their community. Many of these networks show a hierarchy of authority, division of labor and continuity. Criminal organizations are criminal networks that have those characteristics.

Whether a crime is committed by an individual or by a criminal organization partly depends on the nature of the crime. Some crimes cannot be committed by people acting alone, because of their complexity and multi-faceted nature. Whether committing crime is a group or individual activity also depends on the situation and the availability of partners. If the nature of the crime and the situation demand it, and there are willing partners available, the crime may be carried out by a group. This group can be considered to be a criminal network if there is some division of labor (that is, people play different roles and have different duties in carrying out the crime), and the network lasts over time and over more crimes. The latter is important: unless the network lasts beyond a single or limited criminal opportunity, unless the members organize themselves to continue to commit crimes, unless they view themselves as a criminal organization, and unless the network develops durability, reputation, and continuity, it is not a true criminal organization.

Criminal organizations have, to a greater or lesser degree, these characteristics:

- *Sophistication* – what degree of planning is involved for the crimes? How long do criminal ventures last? How much skill and knowledge are required to carry out the crimes?
- *Structure* – is there a division of labor with clearly defined lines of authority and leadership roles?
- *Stability* – does the structure maintain itself over time and over crimes?
- *Self-identification* – do the participants see themselves as being members of a defined organization? Is there, for example, an

emphasis on bonding activities, such as the use of colors, special clothing, language, tattoos, initiation rites, and so on?

• *Authority of reputation* – does the organization have the capacity to force others – both criminals and non-criminals – to do what it wants without resorting to actual physical violence? Does the organization's reputation alone instill fear and intimidate? When Russian mobsters began operating in Brighton Beach in New York City, and disputes arose over territory or shares of the proceeds of a crime, they called in *La Cosa Nostra* to resolve the issue, because it had the necessary authority of reputation.

While criminal organizations exhibit differing degrees of these characteristics, networks totally, or even substantially, lacking them should not be considered true criminal organizations. The greater development that they have, the greater the threat of organized crime they present. At the risk of appearing to be tautological, organized crime could be defined as being crime that is committed by criminal organizations.

Organized crime versus crime that is organized

Let us now turn to what crimes a criminal organization might commit, and especially to how those crimes differ from other crimes. I want to distinguish between crimes that may be extremely complex and highly organized, but which are not committed by criminal organizations, and "true" organized crime. I would call the first "crimes that are organized," and suggest that they are distinct from "organized crime."

For example, in 2003, law enforcement officials in Long Island, New York solved an insurance fraud. The organizers were said to have staged thousands of car accidents and used a network of doctors, lawyers, and others to defraud an insurance company of $48 million.

INVESTIGATORS SAY FRAUD RING STAGED THOUSANDS OF CRASHES

The frauds began with accidents in which a "runner" would recruit friends, relatives, or strangers, promising them $500 apiece for participating. The runner would load them into an inexpensive sturdy American car – usually an aging Cadillac or Lincoln – and drive onto a highway, then veer in front of an unsuspecting driver to cause an accident, usually a fender bender ...

In the confusion, the driver would dart from the car and be ferried away in another automobile, leaving someone else to pose as the driver, in order to avoid being connected to a string of accidents. Sometimes, the getaway car would disgorge people who would later claim to have been in the accident ... .

The passengers then went to one of several counterfeit medical clinics ... that had been set up specifically to treat them ... The clinic management filed no-fault insurance claims and ordered a barrage of tests and procedures, sometimes performing them and sometimes not ...

The clinics were financed by lawyers, accountants and other investors, although doctors [were] listed as the owners.

Each passenger could bring in $50,000 .... [R]unners received $1,500 per "patient" while the "crash dummies" received up to $500 per crash. The lawyers who pressed the claims reaped one-third of the profits, and the clinic managers received another third.

NY Times, August 13, 2003

The grand jury found the perpetrators guilty on 567 indictments. This was clearly a highly-organized crime, involving hundreds of people, clearly defined roles, nearly twenty bogus health care clinics, and a considerable amount of planning and paperwork. It went on for more than two years. But I suggest it was not organized crime. The network was not a criminal organization, with durability and reputation, that had continuity over time and over crimes, and whose members identified themselves as being members of a criminal organization. Its members did not seek to gain monopoly control over their criminal market. They neither used violence nor corrupted public officials. They included doctors, psychiatrists, chiropractors, and dentists – unlikely candidates for gangsters. Other than sophistication and structure, this network seems to have none of the characteristics I identified as characterizing organized crime but instead appears to be a classic case of the opportunistic creation of an entity for the exploitation of a criminal opportunity – entrepreneurship gone haywire as a crime that is organized.

Another example of the distinction comes from the work of Ko-lin Chin on the organization of Chinese human smuggling (Chin, 1998). Chin concluded that the human smuggling he studied was not organized crime, but rather a crime that was organized: "a trade that needs organized participation and execution but it does not appear to be linked with traditional organized crime groups" (Chin, 1998). Other examples of this phenomenon can be found in Natarajan and Belanger's (1998) studies of drug trafficking networks, in which they found opportunistic organizational forms other than those that fit traditional concepts of organized crime, including "freelancers," "family businesses," and "communal businesses." Eck and Gersh (2000) also found that drug trafficking was mostly a "cottage industry" of many small groups – quick to form and quick to break up – rather than large, hierarchically organized distribution networks. Clarke and Brown (2003), with respect to the international trafficking of stolen vehicles, similarly concluded that it was highly likely to be carried out by small groups of entrepreneurs who are "employed in legitimate export businesses or in selling used cars and have discovered that they can exploit their knowledge and contacts to make large profits selling stolen cars overseas." The offenders have to be organized, but they are not organized criminals.

Recalling the importance of reputation in defining organized crime, I believe there is a danger in the promiscuous use of the application of the label "organized crime" to perpetrators of "crimes that are organized," and to criminal networks that lack what should be regarded as the essential defining elements of criminal organizations. This danger was aptly pointed out by the veteran specialists on organized crime, Beare and Martens:

> Bad reputation is a valuable asset that permits criminals access to criminal markets that would, absent this reputation, be closed to them. Victims or potential victims who believe they are confronted by some omnipotent force called organized crime (and most especially mafia) are more fearful, more likely to succumb, and less likely to report to the police. Ironically then, misuse of the labels organized crime and especially mafia – by attaching them to what may be little more than "two-bit" criminal groups – adds to those groups' reputations for violence and actually increases their effectiveness in carrying out crimes. Therefore, law enforcement must not facilitate this perception, and in fact enhance the value of a bad reputation when it is undeserved.
>
> Beare and Martens, 1998:3

Harm

Crime and criminal behavior cause harm and the victims of crime have been harmed in some way by it. They may have been physically hurt, through assault or rape; they may have had their property stolen or destroyed; or they may have been psychologically harmed through fear, intimidation or trauma. Some people are simply fearful of crime, even though they have not been victims of it. Such people, who often live in high-crime neighborhoods behind locked doors, who are afraid to venture out into their neighborhood, who limit their enjoyment of activities such as shopping, going to a movie or visiting friends – are all victims. They are all harmed by crime. Harm, therefore, is very much a part of the concept of crime. It is also very much a part of our concept of organized crime.

Individual criminals can cause harm – even great harm. But in general, individuals acting in concert (such as criminal groups) have a greater capacity for harm than individuals acting alone. These groups may differ in their sophistication, structure, self-identification, and reputation; the characteristics of a criminal organization that I discussed earlier. I would further argue that a criminal organization's capacity for causing harm is a function of these characteristics, together with their size and continuity and that there is a positive correlation: the more of these characteristics an organization has, the greater its capacity for harm, and where-abouts an organization falls on the spectrum of these characteristics determines that capacity.

The harm caused by crime comes in a variety of forms, including economic, physical, psychological, and societal (Maltz, 1990). Criminal organizations cause economic harm when they hijack goods from carriers or warehouses, when they gain monopoly control over certain businesses and thus drive up prices, when they add a so-called "mob tax" to the cost of doing business in areas under their control, and when they undermine the principles of a free market economy. Physical harm from violence (or its threat) comes from extortion, arson, beatings for not repaying loans to loansharks, kidnapping, and, most severely, the murder of rivals or policemen or other public officials such as prosecutors and judges.

Psychological harm flows from physical harm. A credible reputation for violence creates a climate of fear and intimidation. This results in people being unwilling to report crimes to the police, and being unwilling to serve on juries or perform other civic duties. Leoluca Orlando (2001), the former mayor of Palermo, Sicily, described how thoroughly cowed the citizenry of Palermo was by its fear of the Sicilian Mafia. As illustration, Orlando told the story of Vita Rugnetta, who came to a court in Palermo demanding

RESISTING THE MAFIA

Vita Rugnetti was her name. She looked like a character out of a Rossellini movie about Sicily ... her entire world had crashed when she was shown her adored son's dead body, found in the trunk of a car parked in front of police headquarters. Antonino Rugnetta, a low-level Mafioso in training, had been a casualty of the Corleonesi. He had been subjected to the particularly brutal form of murder ... the *incaprettatura* (death of the goat) in which the victim's arms and feet are tied in an arch behind his back with the rope passing around his neck ...

This small woman who stepped into the courtroom asking for justice was dramatically breaking one of the Mafia's oldest taboos. It was possible to turn to another Mafioso for the vendetta if one had been wronged, but *never* to the state. Yet here she was ...

Mrs Rugnetta owned a small furniture shop in one of the narrow alleys of the historic center of Palermo. Her son had supported her, and since his death, this had been her only means of livelihood. But from the day she stepped into the bunker courtroom and asked for justice, she did not sell a single piece of furniture. Nothing ... The *capomafia* of the area had imparted strict orders: nobody was to be a customer at Vita Rugnetta's shop.

Orlando (2001: 112–113)

justice. Years after the trial was over, Vita Rugnetta still sat with her unsold furniture, forced to rely on handouts and other assistance from the few mafia resisters, including Orlando. This fear is insidious and immobilizing; leading to feelings of powerlessness and cynicism about the ability and willingness of government to protect victims, or possible victims, from criminal harm.

Society is harmed by the undermining of its legal and political systems. The political process may be compromised because organized crime pays bribes for public contracts, finances candidates for public office, or even (as in Russia) puts up candidates. This, most corrosive, harm results from the corruption of the legal process and the other institutions of society, and from the undermining of the rule of law. These effects are not likely to be caused by criminals acting alone or by small, unsophisticated criminal groups. They are among the most negative of the impacts of true organized crime.

Transnational organized crime: the new menace

The nature of organized crime changed dramatically during the last quarter of the twentieth century. The expansion of our ideas of what is organized crime can be attributed to a number of factors (see, for example, the *Report of the Committee on Law and Justice*, National Research Council, 1999): first, the globalization of economic activity. By the end of the twentieth century, improvements in transport meant that goods and services moved much more readily across national boundaries than they had done a decade or so before. More importantly, so did people. Business people and travelers had much more contact with other countries, including the multitude of countries in Eastern Europe and the former Soviet Union that had, for generations, been confined behind the Iron Curtain. Second, there was an enormous increase in the number of migrants – including legal migrants, people who were voluntarily smuggled across national borders, and victims of human trafficking, transported by criminals from one country to another. Human smuggling and trafficking have both become highly visible forms of transnational crime. Third, tremendous advances in communications technology made national borders permeable and in some cases irrelevant to impeding or controlling the flow of communications. The use of cell (mobile) phones to communicate with criminal partners, cyber-crimes, identity theft, and the electronic transfer of stolen funds are some examples of how transnational criminals use new technologies. No country can any longer rest secure from transnational crime behind its national borders.

What is transnational crime? The United Nations (1995) defined it as "offenses whose inception, prevention and/or direct effect or indirect effects involved more than one country." This definition seems to include any offenses of any kind, although the specific examples given by the UN include organized crime, corruption, the theft of cultural artifacts, crime associated with migration, trading in human body parts, and environmental crimes. As with other efforts to define organized crime, the concept of *transnational organized crime* (TOC) seems to suffer from the fact that at least some of the qualifying crimes can be committed by individuals, or by groups of individuals who would not count as being a criminal organization. The crimes in question might also include crimes that are organized, but not be organized crime.

The United Nations *Convention against Transnational Organized Crime* (2000) struggled mightily with the definition problem but did ultimately reach agreement on what is an "organized crime group," and what is "transnational crime:"

[A]n organized crime group is a "structured group of three or more persons existing for a period of time and acting in concert with the aim of committing one or more serious crimes or offences in order to obtain, directly or indirectly, a financial or other material benefit." By "serious crime" is meant "conduct constituting a criminal offence punishable by a maximum deprivation of liberty of at least four years or a more serious penalty."

[A]n offence is transnational if "(a) It is committed in more than one state [i.e., country]; (b) It is committed in one state but a substantial part of its preparation, planning, direction or control takes place in another state; (c) It is committed in one state but involves an organized criminal group that engages in criminal activities in more than one state; or (d) It is committed in one state but has substantial effects in another state."

Trends in Organized Crime /Vol. 6, No. 2, Winter 2000, pp. 48–49.

Transnational organized crime on a large scale is a new reality but do not assume that such crime did not exist before the end of the twentieth century. The description above could quite readily have been applied to pirate groups roaming in the sixteenth century. What is different is the scale, the magnitude of the problem, the sophistication of the criminals, and the capacity for harm that some of these transnational criminal organizations have; thus the characterization of transnational organized crime as the "new menace." Much of the discussion in this book will reflect that reality.

What is organized crime? The defining characteristics, which most simply answer the question are, in essence, the ability to use, or a reputation for use of, violence or the threat of violence to facilitate criminal activities, and in certain instances to gain or maintain monopoly control of particular criminal markets. Also essential is the corruption of public officials to assure immunity for its operations, and/or protect its criminal enterprises from competition.

2

Truth, fiction, and myth – the role of popular culture*

Following the widespread media coverage of the arrest of Bernardo Provenzano, *capo di tutti capi* (boss of all the bosses) of the Sicilian Mafia in Corleone, Sicily in April 2006, the columnist Richard Cohen wrote of the symbiotic relationship between the media and the mafia: "When it comes to the Mafia, it's not that life imitates art, it's that they have become indistinguishable" (The Washington Post, April 13, 2006). This intriguing idea, of life, art, and how they pertain to popular culture, organized crime, and the mafia, is the theme of this chapter.

Just about everyone, just about everywhere, has a view of what is organized crime. People think they know what it is, and they almost all have an opinion about who is involved, what gangsters do, and how the mob works. How do they – how do we – know this, and perhaps more importantly, what do we really know?

Relatively few people have direct personal experience or knowledge of organized crime. A very few belong to criminal organizations. Others, a minority, use the services of or buy the goods provided by criminal organizations; obtaining drugs, gambling, borrowing money from a loan shark, or visiting prostitutes –

---

* Thanks are extended to two members of my Organized Crime class at Rutgers University in the Fall 2003, Meghan Kennedy and Meredith Rodriquez, for their assistance with this chapter.

Figure 10 Sicilian Mafia boss Bernardo Provenzano is escorted by a black-hooded police officer as he enters a police building in downtown Palermo, Sicily. Provenzano, who had been on the run since 1963, was captured in a farmhouse near the Mafia power base of Corleone, Sicily in 2006 (AP Photo/Luca Bruno).

acts that might bring them into contact with organized crime. Others grow up or live in neighborhoods where organized crime is present, and therefore can make personal observations. A further minority is those, including me, who are students and academic connoisseurs of the subject: journalists, criminal lawyers, law enforcers, policy makers, students, and scholars. We research, study government reports, and read studies and other serious literature. If other *aficionados* are like me, they also dip into the non-serious stuff as well: novels, movies, television shows, and so on.

What about all the others, the great majority of people? How and what do they know? The public source of information for an array of subjects is mainly the popular media – television, movies, magazines, newspapers, novels, music, video games, and so on. Most of us know what we know about a particular subject because we have seen something about it on television, read something in a newspaper or magazine, saw a movie, or perhaps spoken with someone who has personal experience. Such knowledge is much more likely to be vicarious, rather than direct. Particularly with respect to more "sexy" topics, like organized crime and mafia, this knowledge comes primarily from sources aimed more at entertaining than informing. (Although organized crime is not unique in this respect: the same observation could be made about any number of other subjects.) Accepting the assumption that, for the majority of people, their major sources of information about organized crime are in popular culture, it would be useful to examine some of these sources and the messages they convey. We will consider what seems to be a particular sort of fascination, almost a perverse voyeurism, surrounding the perennially hot topic of organized crime. In this respect, the subject *is* different from others.

Not only do the public media have a profound impact on public perceptions, and both inform and entertain, but it is also significant that they are commercial enterprises. Financial success has to be one of their goals. The packaging and marketing of their products is critical to that financial success. They must capture attention and maintain interest by presenting their information in attractive ways.

"Keeping it simple" is one of the ways of attracting customers. Complex, multi-faceted, subtle messages require more time, effort and resources to deliver and, more importantly, more time and effort to receive. Audiences are much more receptive to messages that are succinct and immediate. Simple, stereotypical messages are especially likely to provide the kind of instant gratification the audience seeks. Under those circumstances, accuracy and objectivity may be in danger. Once a particular image, and the sentiment attached to it, has been accepted by the audience, it is reinforced every time the image is redisplayed. Some experts in organized crime contend that these practices mean that coverage of the subject is superficial and sensationalistic (See, for example, Potter, 1994; Ryan, 1995).

The essence of these experts' complaints is that the media suggest a singular, subjective view of organized crime and market that view through news stories, television, books, and movies. Although this picture of organized crime usually starts in reality, it is skewed through being limited to one particular image or angle. Sensationalistic treatment exaggerates certain aspects of the story while ignoring others, in keeping with the image or angle being promulgated. Mob murders, for example, are much more likely to get headline coverage than a scam involving mobsters putting pressure on stockbrokers to "pump and dump" certain stocks, even though the latter may have much more harmful impact on society.

As well as considering the role of popular culture in spreading certain images of organized crime, we will look at the particular twist given to this image both historically and currently. Specifically, has the emphasis been on the mafia; and has the mafia, and organized crime in general, been romanticized? I contend that the media have stamped a kind of "mafia myth" on the popular imagination. As the NY Times columnist Clyde Haberman noted, the mafia has a "relentless grip ... on popular culture and the news media" (NY Times, March 10, 2006:B1). Beyond pure entertainment value, an over-arching stereotype has been created that may have implications for society's ability to appreciate the threat of organized crime, and combat it.

Given the ubiquitous nature and powerful influence of American popular culture, this particular fascination, the mafia myth, is very likely also to have affected people in other parts of the world. Although I will focus on American cultural influences, I do not mean that the mass media of other countries have not also turned to organized crime as a source of entertainment and fascination. John Dickie (2004:13) describes a very early example: Pietro Mascagni's opera *Cavalleria Rusticana* introduced the story of the Sicilian mafia to the world at its première in Rome on May 17, 1890. Dickie describes this "simple tale of jealousy, honor and vengeance" among Sicilian peasants as:

> [T]he purest, most anodyne form of a myth about Sicily and the mafia, a myth that was something akin to the official ideology of the Sicilian mafia for nearly a century and a half. The mafia was not an organization ... but a sense of defiant pride and honour, rooted deep in the identity of every Sicilian.

This romanticized and compelling mixture of honor, pride, passion, and chivalry hides the dark reality of a murderous and predatory criminal organization that extends from that time to this. *La Piovra*, a popular Italian television series of the 1980s, is a vast and dramatic treatment of the Italian Mafia that demonstrates this enduring portrayal. In the spring of 2006, an Italian television network and a British producer produced a documentary television series, *La Mafia*. Said to be an in-depth look at fifty years of mafia criminal activity, *La Mafia* focused on the "five families" in New York City and the Sicilian Mafia. Recognizing the market value of the mafia label, German and American producers are also involved.

This romanticizing and stereotyping does not only happen in Italy. Underworld figures, young men called *keon-dal*, first appeared in seventeenth-century Korea. They were considered to be shadowy operators and hoodlums (Park, 2001). The *keon-dal* did not cause major harm or victimize ordinary citizens: they valued and honored loyalty and faithfulness, and they sometimes helped the weak and poor. As with the folklore and legend associated with the Sicilian mafiosi, the *keon-dal* have become an attractive source for Korean movie plots, which usually portray them as heroic figures. There is a current belief in Korea that some young men are becoming involved in organized crime because of the romantic views of the *keon-dal* gained from these movies. Life imitates art!

South Africa has urban street gangs, known as *Tsotsi* (roughly a kind of young, street tough). *Tsotsi* was also the title of a 2005 film, based on the well-known South African author Athol Fugard's 1980 novel of the same name. Their message is not of honor and romantic notions of chivalry, unlike the Sicilian and Korean examples. They deal with what it is like to survive in the street, in a sprawling ghetto, under conditions of crushing poverty and discrimination. Violence, hardness, and brutal machismo are pictured as the essential elements for survival, while also showing that qualities such as compassion and understanding still lurk beneath a necessarily thick skin. The lead role – the street gang member – is clearly portrayed as sympathetic. Reaction to this film again demonstrated the appeal of crime and organized crime as subject matter.

These examples give some sense of how the subject of organized crime is presented as entertainment. Popular culture has two forms: entertainment or escapist forms, including fiction, movies, music, television, and video games, and news or information forms, including non-fiction, documentaries, magazines, newspapers, and television and radio news. I am not suggesting that each has equal influence. I am sure, for example, that many more people watch a television crime show or movie than read non-fiction books about organized crime but in some cases, a particular treatment of the subject has a greater impact because it has appeared in many forms.

An example is Mario Puzo's extremely influential novel *The Godfather* (1969) (about which I shall say much more later). The novel was adapted into an enormously successful movie, generated two sequels, and is now available as a video game. The particular picture of the Italian–American mafia presented in these various iterations is regarded as probably the most significant depiction of that subject in any form – at least until the appearance of the television show *The Sopranos*. Marlon Brando, as Don Vito Corleone in *The Godfather* film of 1972, is *the* powerful personification of what a "godfather" looks, talks, and acts like.

The three films are shown over and over, year after year. For millions of viewers, Brando as Corleone *is* the mafia and, even more significantly, he *is* organized crime.

Some cultural forms are geared toward particular audiences and represent the evolving capabilities and reach of the media. Video games are largely attractive to young people, as are certain kinds of music, such as "gangsta rap." Because of the interactive nature of video games, their lasting impressions may be much more powerful than those conveyed by more passive, traditional cultural forms.

How pervasive are the subjects of organized crime and mafia? An Internet search, using various search terms, produced the following results: "organized crime" – 44.8 million hits; "mafia" – 50.8 million hits, "LCN" – 19.5 million hits. "Italian mafia" with 4.6 million hits, trailed behind "Russian mafia" (5.2 million hits) and "Chinese mafia" (4.7 million hits). Searches for different forms of "organized crime" produced hits in the multi-millions for Italian, Russian, Chinese, Japanese, Colombian, and Mexican organized crime. Obviously, there has been much mention of these subjects in the electronic media: "mafia" and "La Cosa Nostra" are especially important trigger words. A mailing from *Insight Media* (Spring 2006), a publication that advertises videos and DVDs for classroom use on criminal justice topics lists four entries under the heading "Organized Crime:" *Mafia: The Inside Story, Organized Crime: A World History* (said to profile "the Sicilian Mafia, considered the gold standard for organized crime"), *The Mafia: An Expose*, and *Modern Mobs* (which in part deals with New York City's "legendary crime families"). The emphasis seems clear. Searches for non-fiction books on the same subjects also show a very definite focus in the coverage:

Number of Nonfiction Books about Organized Crime (OC) in English:

General OC Studies – 126

Italian-American OC (LCN, Mafia) – 92

Italian/Sicilian OC – 31

United Kingdom OC – 10

Russian OC – 6

Asian OC – 14

Other European OC – 5

African OC – 1

Latin American OC – 1

www.wright.edu/~martin.kich/Murder/OCNon.htm

The number of books on the mafia (Italian and Italian-American) dwarfs those on other ethnicities of organized crime groups. This supports my argument about its dominance, although I must mention one caution: this result is only for books written in English. I know that there are a number of books on Russian organized crime written in Russian, and the same is true for Chinese, Italian and Spanish.

Dwight Smith, in his 1975 book, concluded that there had been a "mafia mystique" evident in the United States since the 1950s. There is plenty of evidence that mystique has continued and expanded during the past three decades. Larke (2003:116) traces the fascination back to the US Senate hearings in the 1950s that, he says, "have had a profound influence on subsequent film and television representations of the Mafia." I have described elsewhere the beginning of the US media's fascination with the mafia and the rise of this mafia mystique.

The Birth of the American Mafia Myth?

In 1950–51, a US Senate Committee, chaired by Senator Estes Kefauver of Tennessee, conducted a sweeping examination of organized crime in the United States. The timing of this investigation, with hearings in various US cities, coincided with the early days of television. In part because it was so new, and because there was little regular television programming (unlike the hundreds of channels available today), the televised hearings became great show business. It was this committee and its telecast hearings that, in a massively new way, stamped the image of Italian-American organized crime – of the mafia – on American consciousness. This was not actually the very first time that a criminal organization called the mafia had been covered in the media. But it was the Kefauver committee and its hearings that first put mafia figures on national television. Viewers could see and hear real gangsters for themselves. It was thus the Kefauver committee that made the mafia and organized crime one and the same thing in the minds of the American public.

Television viewers were fascinated by what they saw as a confrontation between good and evil. "Good" was personified by the meek, almost schoolmasterish looks of Senator Kefauver. The bespectacled Tennessean was the common man as hero, a kind of Gary Cooper character from *High Noon*. He stood to do battle with the "evil" personified by a bunch of swarthy Italians and Sicilians named Costello, Adonis, Moretti, Luciano, Genovese, Profaci, and Anastasia, as well as some Jewish hoodlums named Longie Zwillman and Meyer Lansky. White, Anglo-Saxon, Protestant, Middle America was going to the mat with some dark-skinned foreigners who had brought an evil conspiracy to our shores. This was the alien conspiracy theory writ large.

All of the elements of good drama – and of myth – were there. Viewers watched the nervously clenching and unclenching hands of Frank Costello, who refused to permit his face to be televised. He also refused, in a rasping and barely audible voice, to answer questions on advice of counsel. In the minds of the committee members and, of course, in the minds of the viewing public, this confirmed his complicity in the things about which he was being questioned. America, or at least a considerable part of America, reveled in the spectacle of these sweating, fidgeting gangsters professing shocked surprise at being called and questioned, feigning ignorance of any wrongdoing, sometimes being sullenly silent, sometimes refusing to answer, and sometimes evading the questions. These were mafiosi, the masters of the underworld. This was organized crime – or so it seemed ...

The influence of the Kefauver committee in defining organized crime as the mafia was confirmed by a study by John F. Galliher and James A. Cain titled, "Citation Support for the Mafia Myth in Criminology Textbooks." The study examined 20 criminology textbooks with chapters or sections on organized crime that were published in the United States between 1950 and 1972. The most frequently cited source for information about organized crime in these books was the Kefauver committee report, cited in over half the texts, followed by Kefauver's book based on the investigation (Galliher & Cain, 1974). Thus, the image and understanding of organized crime conveyed to students through these textbooks was in large part the image and understanding promulgated by Senator Kefauver and his committee ...

A critic of the "myth-making" by the Kefauver committee is historian William Moore (1974). Moore charged the committee with dramatizing organized crime more than investigating it ... Committee statements and conclusions were seemingly accepted by the public because they fit with their preconceived notions about organized crime. According to Moore, sensationalist journalists and publishers enjoyed a field day, explaining and enlarging on the committee's work; gangster movies and television programs dramatized variations of the same theme. Even after the initial shock and novelty of the Kefauver findings had lifted and critics began to question the more sweeping Committee statements, the public at large continued to hold to the older conspiracy view, thus making more difficult an intelligent appraisal of organized crime.

Kenney & Finckenauer (1995)

The fever of the "field day" has shown little sign of abating in the half century since those sensational hearings. With a few exceptions, the bulk of the media attention to organized crime has focused on the mafia. This is what the public wants to see and read about, and it is this they believe to be "real" organized crime.

From *The Godfather* to *The Sopranos*

Any consideration of popular culture and crime readily establishes that crime in general, and organized crime stories in particular, are well-liked fare. It is clear that most of the public, most of the time, gets most of its information about organized crime from these sources. Among all the images of organized crime portrayed through various media, nothing before or since (until *The Sopranos*) rivaled the impact of Mario Puzo's 1969 blockbuster *The Godfather* and the three movies derived from it. The book and the first movie, featuring the Godfather Don Vito Corleone, were the public "proof" of the mafia's or LCN's existence and structure. This is what organized crime was like; this was the way mobsters looked and lived. It is fair to say that *The Godfather* had more influence on the public mind, and the minds of many public officials, than any library of scholarly works explaining the true nature of organized crime.

How influential was it? According to a former US Federal prosecutor:

> ... the publication and dramatization of *The Godfather* ... did more to alter public perceptions about the American Mafia than any combination of exposes in the past. Before the advent of *The Godfather*, federal courts were very strict about excluding references to the Mafia *per se*, and any prosecutor who was careless in that regard was certain to have a nasty mistrial on his or her

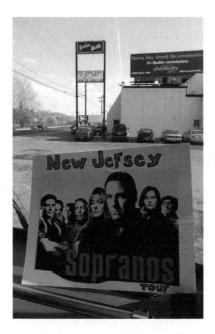

Figure 8 A Sopranos tour sign sits on the dashboard of a tour bus outside the Satin Dolls club, the setting for the "Club Bada Bing" from the HBO series "The Sopranos" (AP Photo/Gino Domenico).

record. Moreover, when jurors were questioned at all about whether they believed in such a thing as organized crime, most were uncertain and the rest were doubters ... After *The Godfather* became so popular, it was the defense attorneys who wanted to ask the questions and assess the extent of the damage – and the extent was really quite substantial. Jurors believe that the Mafia existed, and they had a fixed understanding from Hollywood about exactly how the Mafia operated. That change in public perceptions was important for the courtroom battles which were about to the launched in the latter 1970s.

(Stewart, 2006:76).

Dwight Smith, who reportedly read hundreds of gangster novels while researching his book *The Mafia Mystique*, put Mario Puzo's book at the center of the fictionalized accounts of organized crime that have made it interchangeable with the mafia in the public perception. *The Godfather* was truly a saga of a gangster hero. There had been other gangster heroes in earlier books and movies but, according to Smith, "it was not until Puzo in 1969 that the ethnic traits of 'Mafia' became a permanent part of the basic stereotype patterns that had been established nearly forty years earlier" (Smith, 1975:254). *The Godfather*, Smith said, laid to rest any doubts about the power of ethnicity as the principal character trait for gangsters: "The [American] public was ripe for a book that would ... depict organized crime as an evil, alien, conspiratorial entity comprised of Italians bearing the 'Mafia' label" (1975:277).

Reading an excerpt from *The Godfather* suggests how it depicted the mafia. In this excerpt, Vito Corleone is meeting a man who has come to seek revenge on a couple of young punks who have brutally attacked his daughter. In it, it becomes clear what being "the Godfather" means and how he and the mafia operate outside the normal rules and laws of the larger society (or at least how this occurs in Mario Puzo's imagination).

Don Corleone was gentle, patient. "Why do you fear to give your first allegiance to me?" he said. "You go to the law courts and wait for months. You spend money on lawyers who know full well you are to be made a fool of. You accept judgment from a judge who sells himself like the worst whore in the streets. Years gone by, when you needed money, you went to the banks and paid ruinous interest, waited hat in hand like a beggar while they sniffed around, poked their noses up your very asshole to make sure you could pay them back." The Don paused, his voice became sterner. "But if you had come to me, my purse would have been yours. If you had come to me for justice those scum who ruined your daughter would be weeping bitter tears this day. If by some misfortune an honest man like yourself made enemies they would become my enemies" – the Don raised his arm, finger pointing at Bonasera – "and then, believe me, they would fear you."

(Puzo, 1969:32–33)

This scene illustrates the mafia "client" system of favors, services and dependencies. Power and influence are exercised through knowing the right people in the right places, and through violence when necessary. The first *Godfather* movie, in 1972, was then the biggest money-maker in movie history. Even mafia wannabes copied the style, dress and language of the film's characters. *The Godfather* is still alive and still making an impression on the younger generation, as illustrated by its latest incarnation as a video game:

The Godfather

The Godfather begins in 1936 as the player takes on the role of a low-level Mafia thug working for the Corleone family. To make money for the family, you need to get local shop owners to pay protection ... You can scare them into submission by throwing them through windows, breaking up their stores, aiming a gun at their sensitive points or killing their customers.

Most of the shops are already protected by one of the rival families, and threatening a shop owner can result in prompt action by nearby thugs ... Sometimes I would be able to sneak up behind a thug lurking in an alley and garrote him. A room full of enemies could be cleared with a stick of dynamite or a Molotov cocktail ...

The rise from thug to made man involves outrunning cops, bribing FBI agents, flirting with party girls and throwing mobsters off roofs or into bakers' ovens. Success gains you citywide respect, and the pedestrians who at first insult you as you pass by will later nod pleasantly and even apologize when you bump into them.

Charles Herold, NY Times, April 20, 2006, C12

A contemporary of *The Godfather*, also both a book and a movie, was *The Valachi Papers*; the principal difference being that one was fiction and the other (ostensibly) non-fiction. Peter Maas published his biographical diary of Joseph Valachi in 1968. A mid-level hood, Valachi gave dramatic testimony to the McClellan US Senate Committee Hearings in 1963. Valachi was the first to make the world aware of the label *La Cosa Nostra* "this thing of ours." The movie based on Maas's book came out in 1972. Although neither book nor movie made as great a splash as *The Godfather*, the book was probably at least as widely read by organized crime experts.

Nicolas Pileggi's 1985 book *Wiseguy: A Life in the Mafia* was the basis for the 1990 movie *Goodfellas*. The insider story of mobster Henry Hill, the film starred Ray Liotta, Joe Pesci, and the oft-seen Robert De Niro. Like *The Godfather* series, *Goodfellas* made a significant impact on how the public viewed the mafia but unlike it, *Goodfellas* glorified and romanticized the mafia much less and was much more explicit in depicting not only the benefits of mafia membership, but also its drawbacks. Rather than honor and loyalty, this is a world of treachery and betrayal. Henry Hill demonstrates just how quickly the tables can turn from loyalty to betrayal: perhaps not surprising in a world populated by people whose primary goals in life are money and power, and who have few qualms about just how they achieve them. *Goodfellas* seems to offer proof of the existence of an honest-to-goodness mafia organization, with rules and structures. The movie depicts a mysterious initiation process, a hierarchy, standards of conduct, and a belief system – all of which are theoretically to be followed, although as the movie shows, that is not always the case. *Goodfellas* supports the notion of the mafia as organized crime, but does not glorify it as an attractive alternative lifestyle. For many years, Jerry Capeci covered the New York City LCN families for the New York Daily News and subsequently wrote a book, *The Complete Idiot's Guide to the Mafia* (2005). Asked what was the "truest" movie or television portrayal of mobsters he had ever seen, his answer was "*Goodfellas*, hands down" (NY Times, March 5, 2006).

On January 10, 1999, the television network HBO showed the first episode of a new program, *The Sopranos*. Advertised as a modern depiction of the mafia, the program quickly captured a devoted audience, and its characters became instant pop culture icons. *The Sopranos* shows the mafia in a different light from the images presented in *The Godfather* and *Goodfellas*. It had the traditional and stereotypical mafia imagery, but centered on a dysfunctional New Jersey family whose patriarch, Tony Soprano, happened to be a mob boss. The true or blood family – as opposed to the crime family – was the one with which the public could identify: the characters had a human and personal dimension.

The reach for reality does not mean that *The Sopranos* was free of the clichés and stereotypes typically associated with the mafia. With one exception, all the Soprano crime family members are of Italian descent. Hesh Rabkin, the exception, is Jewish, and as might be expected he functions as *consigliore* (advisor). Tony Soprano's "legitimate" business is waste management, a business notorious for its infiltration by the mafia. Members are "made" in secret, elaborate ceremonies and defectors are punished by death. The macho males of the crime family have hordes of cash stashed away, beautiful young women at their beck and call, a physically intimidating presence, and the power to use violence to get their way. The New Jersey-based Soprano family deals with New York City mobsters, sometimes cooperatively and sometimes combatively. They also maintain connections in the old country, Italy. The intent of *The Sopranos* appears to be to take the traditional, romanticized notion of the mafia and mafiosi, and use it to create a modern version that propagates the standard stereotypes, yet breaks the classic mold. Its mobsters are not polished, mysterious, dark figures, operating in a secret underworld. Outside of their world of crime, they are "ordinary" people, suffering from ordinary problems. They embody the emotions, the attitudes, and the style of very average people – people just like you and me, or almost like you and me.

Asked how true was *The Sopranos*, Jerry Capeci said: "The reel-life gangsters, while conducting their criminal business and in dealings with their relatives and 'comares,' have a real feel to them. They're violent, fly off the handle quickly and are duplicitous double dealers with little or no honor. The dialogue rings true" (The NY Times, March 5, 2006). The quality of the production has also been recognized in its numerous Emmy and Golden Globe awards. *The Sopranos* was the most-watched series ever to air on cable television, averaging between nine and twelve million viewers per episode for six series. Many millions more have watched it on DVD. Combined with all the media attention the show has received, it is very likely that *The Sopranos* will succeed *The Godfather* to become the most influential-ever depiction of the mafia.

As well as stereotyping the mafia, these sorts of television shows and movies have long been accused of negatively stereotyping Italians and creating the impression that all Italian-Americans are members of organized crime groups. Do mafia movies and shows such as *The Sopranos* really affect the image of Italian-Americans? This question was asked of American university students in a class at Purdue University, and the results reported on the *Sicilian Culture* website (www.sicilianculture.com/cinema/impressions.htm). A resounding ninety-eight per cent had seen a television show or movie dealing with the mafia. The most watched included *The Godfather, The Sopranos*, and *Goodfellas*, in that order. Asked if they were fascinated by the mafia lifestyle, ninety per cent of male students and thirty-five per cent of females answered "yes." Asked to name the first famous Italian they could think of, they named Al Pacino, John Gotti, Al Capone, Tony Soprano, Joe Pesci, and Robert De Niro – all either real or "reel" gangsters! For Italians, and people of Italian descent, this has to be depressing.

What is the appeal?

Why is organized crime so common as a subject of popular culture? In his book *Bullets Over Hollywood*, John McCarty argues that "Americans (and I would include most other people as well) admire the antihero gangster because he's an unbound character who goes where he wants, does what he wants and takes no bull from anybody" (Publisher's Weekly, from http://glasgowcrew. tripod.com/ mobbooks.html). There has been a fair amount of armchair philosophizing about the tremendous appeal of mafia-genre movies, television shows, and so on. Vera Dika (2000) claims the films fulfill a white male fantasy of a tribal or homogenous entity built around male bonding. Why this should be limited to white males is not clear, but any reader or viewer will certainly agree that it is very much a male-dominated world that is portrayed. The men eat together, drink together, play cards, or have coffee while talking business, telling crude jokes, or just bullshitting. Women are either sexual objects, or wives, mothers, and sisters, kept in a cocoon-like protected world to care for the house and children, and go to Mass. There is a male camaraderie in the crime families that is usually associated with young men on sports teams, in the military, or in a club or fraternity. George De Stefano (www.then-ation.com/doc/20000207/destafano) suggests that mafia films hark back to "the enduring appeal of the outlaw – the guy who, in a technocratic, impersonal society has the personal power to reward friends, and, more important, whack enemies." Together with the action, sex and violence that are the staple products of the entertainment industry, there is potential for a vicarious response to the kind of "macho" problem-solving practiced by the mafia.

Beyond the visceral, vicarious enjoyment we get from seeing those who have wronged the mafiosi get their comeuppance, lies the thrill that comes from seeing mobsters doing what many of us would like to do, but don't dare. They are not powerless and they do not take any crap from anybody: and that is appealing, as is the

Figure 3 Salvatore Profaci, known as "Sally Pro" and "Jersey Sal," was a major player in the Profaci-Colombo Italian-American crime family of La Cosa Nostra.

mystery associated with any secret organization, ritual and dark deed. The media image of mafiosi is of fast living, beautiful women, sex on demand, luxury cars, drinking, partying, and having plenty of money to throw around without having to work for it. These are elements of a dream life – a fantasy world – for many, especially men and boys, around the world.

Gangsta rap

Gangsta rap is a form of hip hop music. Its main subject is African-American inner city gang life and crime. Since its beginnings in the 1980s, gangsta rap has been controversial largely because it extols (or seems to extol) violence, hatred of gay people and women, racism, and excessive materialism. One of the early gangsta rappers, Ice-T, wrote a song, *Cop Killer*; because of this (and other songs that celebrated violence against the police), law enforcement personnel became very resentful, and the FBI explicitly objected to certain gangsta rap music of that type.

There is a sub-genre of gangsta rap, *mafioso rap*, which, rather than depicting street life in urban ghettos, portrays rappers as rich and successful mobsters. Much of its subject matter comes from mafia films like *The Godfather* and *Goodfellas*, and it idolizes gangsters such as Al Capone, Lucky Luciano, and Frank Costello.

In their study of African-American organized crime, Schatzberg and Kelly said, regarding gangsta rap:

> We see gangster [sic] rap in the modern context of mass media as a vital, invigorating counterpoint to the cultural machinery of the larger society that relentlessly defines and codifies everything about minorities ... The fact that it chooses an organized crime term, gangster, to define itself is also instructive. In the ghetto, it is the gangster, the outlaw, who defines the oppressive forces and manages to survive without groveling in the dust and submitting to racism.

> Schatzberg & Kelly, (1997:254–256)

Cultural resistance to the mafia

If popular culture is so powerful in spreading images that exalt and idealize the mafia, is it possible to harness its power to counter and combat these images? If films, popular music, and television both reflect and contribute to behavioral standards, can their messages reinforce the values that make for law abiding, value-oriented citizenship? Many believe they can, and that the potential positive influence of popular culture should not be underestimated (See *Trends in Organized Crime*, Winter 1998).

Supporters of the idea of using popular culture to resist and combat the mafia do not see it as a job for the government: government use of the media to relay its message is usually associated with propaganda. Government leaders and officials can, however, be players in and even catalysts for ways of pushing back against organized crime through the media. But it is the leaders of civil society – artists, writers, musicians, producers, directors, and editors – who must take up this task. This has happened in the very home of the mafia – Sicily, where one isolated official, the Mayor of Palermo, was mainly responsible for building and fanning the fires of resistance.

To make sense of a complex story in a relatively short time, it is perhaps best to use that mayor's own words. When Leoluca Orlando was growing up in Palermo, Sicily was in the grip of a particularly vicious mafia sect centered in Corleone. (That Mario Puzo gave his "godfather" character the name "Corleone" is certainly not coincidental.) As a law student, then as a councillor, and finally as Mayor of Palermo, Orlando made fighting the mafia his life's work. He tells his story and sets forth his views about culture and the mafia in his book, *Fighting the Mafia* (2001).

Orlando energized teachers, mothers, and especially children to reject the historical Sicilian acquiescence to the mafia. They were encouraged to turn away from sheep-like acceptance of mafia domination and to speak and act. This was risky behavior – especially for Orlando. Nevertheless, he and his followers and believers persisted. As a result, the citizens of Palermo have made giant steps in taking back their city from the mafia. Whether this effort will succeed in producing long-lasting reform remains to be seen. Success will depend on the permanence of a culture of lawfulness, in contrast to the culture of deviance that has dominated Sicily for hundreds of years.

FIGHTING THE MAFIA

... [O]ur struggle showed that the law court is only one front in the campaign against violence and lawlessness. The other is culture. An image that occurred to me early in my own fight against the Mafia was of a cart with two wheels, one law enforcement and the other culture. If one wheel turned without the other, the cart would go in circles. If both turned together, the cart would go forward.

So, at the same time as brave lawmen and prosecutors were dying in order to establish a rule of law, we were trying to rebuild our civic life ... reclaiming our children and their future ... We began to implement an anti-mafia curriculum ....

We also began to work with the children in the "Adopt a Monument" program ... In the last few years, some 25,000 students have adopted over 160 monuments in Palermo: churches with murals to be uncovered ... parks to be made green and blooming again.

Leoluca Orlando, *Fighting the Mafia*, 2001:6–7.

Building partly on the tactics and experience of the Palermo renaissance, activists, advocates and scholars in different countries have modified some of what was done in Palermo for other world trouble spots. Under the auspices of the Washington-based National Strategy Information Center, a *Culture of Lawfulness* (COL) school course has been developed. This course, which has versions for both younger and older students, has been taught in hundreds of schools to thousands of students in Mexico and has been offered in schools in the former Soviet Republic of Georgia, the United States, Lebanon, and soon in Panama. It has also been adapted for police training in Mexico, Colombia, and Panama.

COL was designed to challenge the acceptance of the domination of organized crime as inevitable, and to instill respect for and belief in the rule of law and the importance of civil society in resisting and combating crime and corruption. One of the "visual aids" shown to the students in all the countries using the course is *Goodfellas*, chosen for its stark and unvarnished depiction of the harsh realities of life in the mafia. The hope is that the reality depicted in the movie – in conjunction with other features of the course – will at least make the youngsters think, and perhaps deter them from pursuing what they may regard as a glamorous, exciting, and lucrative life as a gang member and mob wannabe.

COL is intended to be one part of a three-pronged effort to build a cultural bulwark against organized crime. The second prong comprises the institutions of moral authority – for example, churches, mosques, and synagogues. From the Sicilian experience, religious institutions must take a leading position in assuming the high moral ground and opposing the mafia.

The third prong is encouraging – especially newspapers and television – to shine the glare of a searchlight on the evils perpetrated by criminal organizations. This means editorials that condemn crime and corruption wherever they are found, investigative reporting that exposes criminals, and those who collude with them, especially politicians, and highlighting the heroic efforts of crime fighters at all levels. The idea is to shift the mantle of heroism from the shoulders of mobsters and gangsters to the shoulders of those who risk their lives to fight crime – police, investigators, prosecutors, and judges.

As of the time of writing, this three-pronged effort is only being fully pursued in Palermo. The biggest obstacle is to find new Leoluca Orlandos, charismatic and idealistic leaders, who are courageous and bold enough to risk their lives in fighting the mafia.

Myths, organized crime, and the mafia

Having made much of the myth of the mafia, I want to address the question of why we should care. First, I need to outline what myths are and how they might work in this context. "Myth" is often loosely used to refer to something that is untrue, yet is believed as if it were true. Beliefs in ideas or phenomena that have no (or only a very partial) factual basis are quite common. For example, in the world of crime, many believe that (contrary to the actual data) the elderly are at a high risk of being victims of crime, or (again without any supporting data) that the death penalty is a deterrent to murder. These are just like the belief that organized crime is all (and only) about Italians belonging to something called "the Mafia." Myths, and the myth-based thinking they give birth to, play a part in shaping both popular and official views, and consequently influence public policies. How a problem is defined obviously influences any proposed solution. It is therefore important to consider the myths that may shape our perceptions of organized crime.

Myths reduce complex problems to simple terms and propositions, and help give meaning and direction to reality. Once we believe a particular myth, however, we tend to accept, modify, or reject new information depending on how well it fits that myth. Thus, new knowledge or factual evidence will not necessarily dispel a belief in a myth. What is wrong with myth-based thinking? As well as its dubious foundations, the danger is that once a myth is believed, skepticism disappears and the myth influences our thinking, and then our acting, as if it were a fact. Myth becomes the basis for action. The result is actions that are patently wrong, and actions that would not otherwise be taken. To draw a horrific example from the past, Nazi propaganda (using myths and stereotypes) about the Jews both fed and escalated latent anti-Semitism to the point of justifying their elimination. Although much less dramatic and far smaller in scope, the case of the 1890 murder of the New Orleans Police Chief, Hennessey, is also directly related to the mafia myth. Italian extortion rings victimizing the Sicilian-American community operated in New Orleans at that time. There was a public outcry against "an international secret criminal organization called the Mafia," seen as behind the Hennessey assassination, a combination of fact and prejudice that meant many people were ready to believe the myth. When nine of the original suspects were acquitted, an angry lynch mob stormed the jail where some of the suspects (all Italians) were being held and killed eleven people.

Besides such extreme examples, myth-based public policies – policies intended to solve social problems – that are based on false understanding and explanation are much more likely to fail than succeed. When the FBI first began looking into Russian organized crime in the United States, they largely did so through the prism of their experience and knowledge of *La Cosa Nostra*. Assuming that other ethnically-based organized crime would look like LCN, they searched for hierarchical structures, godfathers, and so on. They did not find them; although in some cases, with media help, they created "godfathers." It took some time, and progress was made only in fits and starts, before understanding of the structure of Russian émigré crime (with floating network structures and relatively flat hierarchies) dispelled the Russian mafia myth and enabled the Bureau to focus on the actual problem. The result of such policy failures is the waste of time and resources, and the disillusionment of policy makers and the public. In the end, the problem is not only left unsolved, but may be worse than before anything was done.

In the early 1970s, the British criminologist Stanley Cohen discussed "moral panics" (Cohen, 1972). A moral panic, he said, is an exaggeration or distortion of some behavior perceived as deviant or criminal. This distortion is mostly created by the media:

[A] ... group of people emerges to become defined as a threat to societal values and interests; its nature is presented in a stylized and stereotypical fashion by the mass media ... Sometimes the panic passes [but] at other times it has more serious and long lasting repercussions and might produce such changes as those in legal and social policy ...

Cohen, (1990:9)

Although "panic" might be too strong a word to describe what has happened with the Italian mafia, exaggeration, distortion, and stereotyping have certainly been present, as have been the repercussions.

I would contend that popular culture's exaggerated focus on the Italian-American mafia and the impact of that focus on public perceptions has led to the ignoring of or actually aiding other organized crime threats – in which criminal organizations that did not "seem" like the mafia were overlooked, the skewing of the tools and policies for combating organized crime – *viz.* the FBI and Russian organized crime, the inflation of the roles of some common criminals by loosely applying the "mafia" label, and the negative stereotyping of many honest and hard-working Italian immigrants and their descendants – "if they are Italians they must have something to do with the mafia." I am not suggesting that the media have consciously set out to do these things, but that their attempts to inform and entertain – especially to entertain – have led to some of the results. I also do not, as I have repeatedly said, deny an Italian mafia exists. My argument is that we need a more comprehensive and multi-faceted picture of organized crime, which is in keeping with reality. Such a picture would better portray the serious harm that criminal organizations of all kinds commit and that affect all of us. Given its critical role, it is up to popular culture, in all its forms, to paint that picture.

3
Explaining the past, present, and possible future*

Because they are made up of people, criminal organizations (and therefore organized crime), like many social constructs, show considerable variety and substantial diversity. These present an enormous challenge to our efforts to come up with a complete explanation or a comprehensive theory that will explain, and help us to understand, all criminal organizations and all organized crime.

Theory and explanation

Although it may seem basic, it will be helpful to be clear on what I mean by "a theory." A theory is postulated in an effort to explain a real world phenomenon. Theories organize what we know (or think we know at a particular time) about a question or issue, and answer questions about why something is the way it appears to be. A theory uses different forms of information – descriptive, comparative, and explanatory – to perform its functions. Theories describe, and provide a context within the real world, by taking

* Thanks are extended to members of my Organized Crime class at Rutgers University in the Fall 2002 for their assistance with this chapter. Specific gratitude is due to Kristopher Arnold, Heather Buchanan and Melissa D'Arcy.

into account what is known about the phenomenon in question. However, the most important function of a theory is the explanatory: explaining and interpreting the apparent relationships among observed phenomena. On the foundation of the explanatory function, theories also have a predictive function; they make predictions about future relations among events possible. Finally, theories have a control or influencing function; they suggest steps or directions for controlling or altering the relations among events. Thus, we can use theories as a basis for trying to alter what we predict will happen. This is important, because understanding why a particular organized crime situation exists becomes a basis for combating that situation. By helping us to organize what we know, theories make the important contribution of serving as heuristic devices; that is, they stimulate and guide further investigations and discoveries.

So, let us look at some of the most popular attempts at explanations – past and present – of organized crime. Some, as you will see, have been a lot more successful than others. We'll begin with an old standby, the "alien conspiracy" theory.

Alien and other conspiracies

US history exemplifies quite well the idea that a country's organized crime problem results from infiltration by a group of alien foreigners. Beginning in the 1800s, first the Irish, and then most commonly the Italians (and particularly Sicilians), were believed to have invaded and infiltrated an otherwise law-abiding America. The Italians were believed to have formed a highly structured, secret, nationwide criminal organization: "The Mafia." Nearly two centuries later, similar beliefs and stereotypes developed in Western Europe about "criminal hordes" invading from the East after the collapse of the Berlin Wall in 1989 and the Soviet Union in 1991. This can only loosely be called theorizing, but such loose theories often become popular myth, as they did in the US. Such a theory of organized crime is, at best, very tenuous. In the US today, this explanation is largely discredited. Although a "mafia myth" persists, most experts agree that the Mafia, *La Cosa Nostra*, and organized crime are not synonymous. This is not to deny the existence of these forms of criminal organizations, but rather their exclusivity and monopoly.

The alien conspiracy notion suggests that the crimes and the criminal behaviors of organized crime in the United States originated elsewhere; an international conspiracy in which members of the Sicilian Mafia brought their crimes and their criminal traditions to the United States in the late 1800s and early 1900s. They were transplanted, bag and baggage. Once in the US, these criminal invaders organized themselves in a highly rational and orderly manner, creating a national "Mafia Commission", which dictated local policies to all crime "families" around the country and controlled all organized crime in the United States. Their structure was believed to be a highly organized hierarchy with clearly delineated roles and functions.

However, the explanatory power of the alien conspiracy theory is quite poor. First, if organized crime originated with the Sicilian/Italian immigration, there should have been little or no such crime in the United States before then. However, historical records show this was clearly not the case; numerous studies have demonstrated that organized crime existed in white Protestant, Irish, Jewish, and other communities (see, for example, English, 2005) well before the arrival of the Italians. Second, if this was purely an exclusively Italian phenomenon, other ethnic groups should not have been involved, but this was clearly not the case. Ethnic diversity, and the number of independent criminal entrepreneurs, refutes the notion of a mafia with a total national control of all organized crime. Third, if organized crime were a transplant, mafia operations in Sicily and the United States ought to have been similar, but this was also not the case. Mafiosi in Sicily and southern Italy were (and to some extent still are) integral parts of the social system. They have significant economic and political roles that go well beyond the strictly criminal (see Paoli, 2003; Schneider & Schneider, 2003). Such dominance has never existed in the United States, where their role has been almost exclusively criminal, based on the fear produced by their use (or threatened use) of violence, and on corruption. Finally, has the alien conspiracy theory any heuristic value? On the contrary, acceptance and adoption of this explanation and its attendant myth of the mafia served to discourage research and investigation rather than encourage it. It became more an ideology than a theory. Myth and ideology tend to be close-minded rather than open-minded influences, accepting only confirming evidence. Cynics were generally not welcome to examine the tenets of the alien conspiracy. Therefore, research to test the theory was impossible, because it was seen as neither desirable nor necessary.

Conspiracy (as opposed to "alien conspiracy") does play a part in helping to describe and explain, and possibly predict and control, organized crime. As with other crimes, the provision of illicit goods and services involves the crime of conspiracy when two or more people carry it out in an organized manner. By definition, people who organize to violate the law, that is to engage in organized crime, are engaging in a criminal conspiracy. The fact that conspiracy is itself a crime underlies the "crime" part of the explanation, but who conspires with whom, and under what circumstances, underlies the "criminal behavior" part. If there has to be a criminal conspiracy for there to be organized crime, then conspiracy must be taken into account, but this is not a theory. Conspiracy does have a value in stimulating the question of who the conspirators are and on what basis they decide to conspire.

In the context of alien conspiracies, it is interesting to note that this characterization also came to be applied to the Chinese and Russian "Mafias" (see Posner, 1988; Finckenauer & Waring, 1998), and to the Japanese *Yakuza* (Kaplan & Dubro, 1986). In the

US, and in the Western European experience, belief in alien conspiracies reflects a need to blame others for one's own problems – to find scapegoats – as well as the powerful desire to find simple answers to complex problems. This way of "explaining" dies hard; as is reflected by some of the same kind of alien conspiracy theory thinking emerging in the context of the current war against terrorism.

Cultural climates for organized crime

Cultural transmission

Among the myriad efforts to explain crime, sociologists such as Shaw and McKay (1942), Miller (1958), and Schrag (1971) have suggested that offenders (in their descriptions, lower-class young people living in slum conditions) break the law because they adhere to a unique and independent value system that exists in, and is the product of, the lower socio-economic class slum areas of major cities. This value system, these authors said, is different from the middle-class value system and in conflict with it. Furthermore, this criminally-oriented value system and its traditions are passed down from generation to generation in cultural transmission.

Further work, in the years since this explanation of crime was first postulated, shows that the criminal values that are learned through cultural transmission are not restricted to city slums or to the lower classes. Wherever and whenever young people grow up in areas where there is a considerable amount of gambling, prostitution, drug trafficking, loan-sharking, the numbers racket (a form of illegal lottery), and extortion; where there are successful criminal role models pursuing these activities; where there is intimate personal contact between the young people and the successful criminals; and where there is a prevailing atmosphere of contempt for and disregard of the law, there is a special vulnerability to recruitment into crime and, specifically, into organized crime.

The known practices of organized crime groups in attracting and recruiting youngsters from urban street gangs supports the validity of this explanation.

Cultural conflict

Conflict has also been alleged to be the stage on which crime, and organized crime, can be seen (see, for example, Sellin, 1938). As cultures come into contact, in an increasingly more complex and pluralistic society, the stage is set for inter-cultural and inter-group conflict. People may be expected to conform not only to the values of the larger society in which they live but also to the values of their own culture. Where these are different – where they are in conflict – the person is torn. This is especially true for the second generation of migrants, the children of immigrants.

Cultural conflict is most common after migration from one country to another or from one area of a country to another. The values of the old country or area may have sanctioned certain kinds of behavior, whereas the laws of the new country may outlaw that behavior. Because the United States is a country of migrants, the potential for cultural conflict and ensuing crime is especially high there, but the same is increasingly true of many other countries in the world. The global development of economies, and the increased pressure and/or ability to move from one place to another, has enormously increased migration: millions of people are on the move.

Cultural conflict offers one explanation for the involvement of members of some migrant groups in organized crime. Cultural values, traditions, or behaviors brought to the new country may conflict with the values, traditions, and behaviors prevailing there. Migrants are outsiders, excluded from jobs and other legitimate opportunities; they do not speak the language and they cluster in neighborhoods with others who share their background and culture. These neighborhoods can then become ripe recruiting grounds for street gangs that are the farms for criminal organizations. They are also rich in opportunities for victimizing the ignorant and naïve.

Strain between ends and means

The "strain" theory explanation views crime as resulting from the frustration and anger people feel over their inability to achieve legitimate social and financial success. Unlike cultural transmission theories, in this theory, people are believed to share similar values and goals but the chances of reaching their goals are believed to be either enhanced or limited by their particular socio-economic class. In lower-class slum areas, legitimate avenues to success are closed or severely limited. Where acceptable means for obtaining success do not exist, people may either use deviant means or may reject societal goals and substitute others. Merton (1957) described American society as stressing the goals of wealth, success, and power. The socially-permissible means for achieving these goals have always been hard work, education, and thrift but the opportunity for reaching them is very much shaped by social class and status. Those with little formal education and few economic resources find that they are denied the opportunity legally to acquire money and other symbols of success. This is the strain. One response may be the development of criminal solutions to the problem: "A cardinal American virtue, ambition," said Merton, "promotes a cardinal American vice, deviant behavior" (1957:146).

Cloward and Ohlin (1960) took this idea one step further. They agreed with Merton that socio-economic class membership controls access to legitimate means of achieving social goals, but they went beyond this to state that illegitimate means for goal attainment were also unevenly distributed and thus unevenly available. Some lower-class neighborhoods provide more opportunities for illegal gain, in access to rackets and other organized crimes, than do others. Thus, there is a possible connection with organized crime. Opportunities for illegal success are said to be present in areas where "stable patterns of accommodation" exist between the criminal world and the conventional. In these areas, adult criminals have developed relationships with businesses and, through bribery and corruption, with the police and other criminal justice officials, so they are immune from arrest and prosecution. Their criminal activities – drugs, gambling, loan-sharking, prostitution – provide a relatively stable, and perhaps substantial, income and, most importantly, an alternative means to the goals of money, power, and status. Under the tutelage of adult criminals, young people in these areas are recruited into a criminal subculture. In this view, lower-class urban young people join gangs specializing in theft, extortion, and so on. Later, they become part of the adult criminal organizations. Just as some youngsters learn to become bankers, lawyers, or businesspeople, others learn to become professional burglars, numbers runners, bookies, or fences. Furthermore, they learn how to build strong political ties and the importance of hiring the best lawyers to avoid prosecution and conviction. Crime in general, and organized crime in particular, is simply an alternate route to upward mobility.

Successful criminal organizations demonstrate to these young people that crime does pay. Organized crime can be seen as attractive, natural, and relatively painless. Its presence demonstrates the corruption of politicians and the police. Respect for, commitment to, and belief in the moral validity of law are diminished by this demonstration. This makes it very difficult for parents to teach their children that the way to get ahead is through hard, honest, labor. The damaging economic effects of numbers rackets, drugs, and so on reduce even further the economic viability of the afflicted neighborhoods. Already sparse legitimate opportunities become even more limited and even less available, and there may be even less to lose if convicted of a crime (Cressey, 1970). The proliferation of urban street gangs in certain cities in the United

States has been explained by such factors as limited access to social opportunities, social disorganization in many urban neighborhoods, concentrations of poverty, a predominance of female-headed households, unemployment, discrimination, and racism (see, for example, Alejandro A. Alonso's research: www.streetgangs.com/research). Strain as an explanatory factor in criminal behavior seems not only to be true in the US. In their exhaustive examination of international crime and crime-related data, van Dijk and Kankaspunta (2000) concluded that strain and relative deprivation were important factors in crime in many different countries.

Each of the above explanations approaches organized crime in a slightly different way, but they share many similarities. First, that poor urban neighborhoods provide a fertile environment for the cultivation and growth of crime in general and organized crime in particular; second, that choosing to become involved in this kind of criminal behavior results from a choice between what are seen as less desirable alternatives. To some degree, this is a forced choice, because no attractive alternatives are available. Studies of international crime have determined that urbanization, economic strain (young men dissatisfied with their income), and lifestyles that involve much risk-taking behavior account for a considerable amount of criminal victimization (van Dijk, 1999).

Poor urban neighborhoods often have a variety of ethnic groups and newly arrived migrants. So, let us now turn to the possible relationship between ethnicity and organized crime.

Ethnicity and ethnic succession

Beginning with the work of Daniel Bell (1953), Francis Ianni (1972, 1974), and later James M. O'Kane (1992), organized crime in the United States in particular has been described as being "caused" by the efforts of successive migrant groups to "make it." According to this explanation, migrants, cut off from legitimate opportunities for achieving socio-economic and political success, are forced by circumstances to climb what Bell called the "queer ladder" of upward social mobility: crime, and especially organized crime. Ianni advanced this explanation of ethnicity's role in organized crime by proposing the notion of "ethnic succession." This comes about, he said, as one ethnic group replaces another on the queer ladder of mobility, and the preceding groups move on to social respectability (and presumably out of organized crime). Thus, in US history, the Irish were replaced by the Jews, who were in turn replaced by the Italians, who in turn were replaced by African Americans, and so on. This was not only true in the US, as witnessed in the work of Kelly (1986), who reflected on the important role attributed to ethnicity in describing a study of Jews who migrated to Israel from the then-Soviet Republic of Georgia. That study, he said:

> ... shows the relationships between ethnicity and organized crime; it reveals the dilemma ethnic groups not fully acculturated into their host society face: how does one gain acceptance and approval when the traditional routes to these desired goals are either closed off or sharply circumscribed by cultural values within the ethnic group?

There are several major problems in using ethnicity as a general explanation of organized crime. One is that ethnicity is not by itself the proximate cause of organized criminal behavior. The difficult socio-economic circumstances ethnic migrants (and also non-migrant ethnic minorities) find themselves in may explain their potential vulnerability to this kind of criminality. If it is so, any socio-economically disadvantaged individuals and groups should be prime candidates for recruitment into organized crime. Ethnicity would then be a secondary attribute characterizing some of these individuals and groups, meaning we should find non-ethnic as well as ethnic organized criminal groups, which we do. The ethnicity theory cannot account for the emergence of non-ethnic groups in organized crime, such as certain outlaw motorcycle gangs and even some prison gangs. Although some of these particular crime groups have clear ethnic identifications, others do not. They may, however, share certain other characteristics historically associated with ethnic migrants: namely alienation, distrust, fear, and discrimination.

Another limit to the ethnic explanation is the obvious point that not all nor even most members of ethnic groups, nor most migrants, become members of criminal organizations or commit other crimes. Therefore, ethnicity cannot be a "cause" of organized crime. Further, contrary to the notion of ethnic succession, emergence of other organized crime groups has not necessarily resulted in the displacement of earlier groups. This was particularly true of the Italians in the United States, who have survived years of competition from a variety of other criminal organizations.

If ethnicity is not the cause of organized crime, then a theory of ethnicity cannot be a comprehensive theory of organized crime. I agree with Albini (1988) that "ethnicity must be viewed as a variable that becomes significant only when it is found in combination with a host of other variables that seek to explain the complex puzzle of organized criminal involvement" (pp. 347–348).

Many of the causal factors identified by the proponents of cultural transmission, strain, and cultural conflict are also found in the work of ethnicity theorists, as these factors frequently exist in conjunction with ethnic identification. As well as sharing ethnicity, potential criminals with particular ethnic backgrounds often share other characteristics that are especially (but not exclusively) associated with new migrants. Living in socially disorganized neighborhoods, being poor, suffering language problems, or being unskilled or uneducated all limit the access to and the ability to take advantage of legitimate opportunities. And all of these characteristics have been said to be linked to the cause of crime. Ethnicity is compounded with other variables, and it is difficult, if not impossible, to sort out its individual and special effects.

Lupsha (1981) and Fox (1989) claimed that there is little causal relationship between ethnicity and organized crime:

> ... to stress ethnicity may obscure the individual gangsters and the options available to them ... [Organized crime] derived less from social conditions or difficult childhoods or there-but-for-fortune bad luck than from a durable human condition: the dark, strong pull of selfish, greedy, impatient, unscrupulous ambition.

> Fox, (p. 76).

Ethnicity does have a role in explaining organized crime, but neither does it necessarily work alone nor in the way some theorists have proposed. The last years of the twentieth century saw a host of civil conflicts around the world, in such far-flung places as Rwanda, East Timor, Haiti, and the former Yugoslavia, among others. These conflicts were, at least partly, based on ethnic differences and ethnic cleansing featured in many of them. Crime, and organized crime in particular, was also greatly entangled or intertwined in these conflicts, especially in Bosnia, Croatia, and Serbia (all former Yugoslav states), and in Albania. These states have all been sources of organized crime from the 1990s. Phil Williams argues that "ethnic conflicts have significant implications for transnational criminal and terrorist activities" (1999:46). Among the implications he cites for organized crime are that ethnic conflicts:

- provide an incentive for criminal activity to fund political struggle – for example, arms for drugs deals;
- create and perpetuate hatreds that transcend national boundaries and thus increase the potential threat of transnational organized crime;
- spawn large numbers of well-trained specialists in violence with knowledge and expertise that can be used by criminal organizations.

These developments indicate that ethnicity cannot be ignored when trying to explain and understand organized crime. However, we should heed Jay Albanese's (1996) warning and avoid the "ethnicity trap" that simply stereotypes certain ethnic groups as being criminal, without accounting for the prevailing economic, social, and political conditions, legitimate and illegitimate opportunities, and the other factors that may operate in conjunction with and provide a context for ethnicity. Only by taking account of these possible contexts can we find more theoretically-sound explanations. This caution applies not only to the ethnicity and ethnic succession theories, but also to the idea of the alien conspiracy.

Enterprise theory

Turning away for the moment from whom particular criminals might be, and why they might have become involved in criminal organizations, we'll look at what kinds of criminal endeavors these organizations choose to exploit and why. Enterprise theory proposes that illicit entrepreneurs exist because the legitimate marketplace leaves potential customers for goods and services unserved, or unsatisfied (Smith, 1980). This explanation of organized crime has been developed more recently by, among others, R. Thomas Naylor (1997). Naylor describes enterprise crimes as the specialty of criminal organizations. Those crimes involve the production and distribution of "new" goods and services through complex market relationships between suppliers and customers, and merchants and financiers. The transactions in which these goods and services are bought and sold are voluntary; the customers demand and willingly seek the goods and services offered.

In the original exposition by Smith, enterprise theory stipulated that enterprises range across a spectrum that includes legitimate businesses and certain kinds of crime. Any business can be conducted across the spectrum of behavior, and legality is an arbitrary point on that spectrum, which new laws or regulations can shift. Moving the point of legality does not necessarily change behavior; it may simply make illegal behavior that was formerly legal – or vice versa. The American experience of Prohibition is a prime example of the spectrum of enterprise. When the 18th Amendment to the US Constitution, and the Volstead Act of 1920, set conditions on the distribution and consumption of alcohol, they did not really affect the demand nor change the technology for producing alcohol, but they did create illegal markets and produce the conditions for the formation of large criminal enterprises. According to Fox:

> Organized crime in America was permanently transformed by thirteen years of Prohibition. The old, clear line between underworld and upperworld became vague and easily crossed. With so many Americans casually defying the law, gangsters took on an oblique legitimacy .... Crime was nationalized by Prohibition, as most of the men who would dominate organized crime for the next three or four decades got their start as bootleggers.

> Fox, (1989:51)

High demand for a particular form of goods (such as drugs) or services (such as gambling) that are illegal, combined with a relatively low level of risk of arrest and very high profits, provides "ideal conditions for illicit business groups to enter the market to seek profits by organizing the supply" (Lodhi & Vaz, 1980:145). Just as there is a spectrum of entrepreneurship, there is also a spectrum of customers, including customers whose legitimate needs are met legally. On the illegal side are customers whose legitimate needs are not met for some reason, customers with illicit needs or demands, and extortionists who exploit the domains of other entrepreneurs. The latter, according to Schelling (1971), are engaged in the "true" business of organized crime: extortionate monopoly.

Whether the products are illegally produced but legal goods or services or illegal goods and services, there must be a market for them. A certain rate of consumption must be maintained to justify the risk and to produce a profit. Just as in legitimate businesses, the usual way to expand profits is to expand the market. Competition must be discouraged and eliminated. Recognizing that while certain unsavory and illegal practices such as violence, corruption, and extortion are used to develop, maintain, control, and expand these markets, the organized criminal is, nevertheless, principally a businessperson, albeit an illegal one.

Enterprise theory employs propositions taken from the economic laws of supply and demand so its ability to describe, explain, and predict organized crime can be tested using these propositions. Drugs – in certain forms and in certain circumstances – are illegal. There is a substantial demand for illegal drugs, creating a market for organized crime in which huge profits can be made. Suppose the government legalized drugs, as some people advocate; shifting the demarcation point on the spectrum that divides legal drugs from illegal? If the necessary controls and conditions in place, what would be the effect on supply? If people wanting drugs could go into a clinic, or drugstore and buy them for less than they had paid in the illegal market, what would happen to the illegal suppliers? Or suppose a tremendously effective form of public education and drug prevention drastically reduced demand: what would be the effect? Both suppositions would alter the market conditions under which the lucrative drug market is being exploited by organized crime. Although I have oversimplified these examples, they nevertheless illustrate the potential applications of enterprise theory for public policy.

As organized crime has become more and more transnational, researchers are paying attention to how transnational criminal organizations organize criminal markets in ways consistent with enterprise theory. Adamoli, et al. (1998) point out a category of offenses driven by supply and demand, involving either the movement of goods like drugs, arms, stolen cars, waste, and nuclear materials, or services like prostitution and human trafficking across national boundaries. These goods and services are all either illegal, regulated or in short supply, thus their markets might be influenced by legalization, changes in regulation, or increase in supply. A second category of crimes indicated by Adamoli, et al., involves the exploitation of resources, such as fraud and computer crimes. The first category includes more traditional organized crimes, while the second covers economic and white-collar crimes. Rather than involving the creation of illicit enterprises along the lines of legitimate businesses, this second category involves the penetration of the legitimate sector for criminal purposes.

Where are these criminal enterprises? Current organized crime hotspots are the Golden Triangle in East Asia (drugs and human smuggling and trafficking), the former Soviet Union and Eastern Europe (all forms of smuggling and trafficking, fraud, corruption, and money laundering), Colombia and Mexico (drug trafficking, and human trafficking and smuggling), and Southern and Eastern Africa (fraud and corruption, drug and arms trafficking, and money laundering).

Implications for the who, how, and what of organized crime

How might we integrate these explanations into a more comprehensive understanding of organized crime? Ethnic factors might define a pool of possible recruits to organized crime, and provide a way of insuring the trust and kinship necessary for collaboration, but there may be a number of other issues related to ethnicity, and to conspiracy.

These considerations raise the question of indigenous criminality versus imported: do newly-arrived, formerly law-abiding émigrés become criminals because of the force of limited circumstances? This is cultural conflict and strain. Or were they already criminals in their country of origin? Were there possibly also co-conspirators? The answers to these questions have implications for both the ethnic and the cultural explanations of organized crime. Other related issues pertain to the phenomenon of within-group victimization – some ethnic groups, for example, the Chinese, seem particularly to victimize their fellows, the issue of limited socio-economic mobility for newly-arrived ethnic groups, which precipitates their involvement in organized crime, and the role of feelings of distrust, fear, lack of respect, and general ignorance of the customs and systems of their new homeland that may be particularly prevalent in specific ethnic groups.

Having decided they will engage in crime and with whom they will do it, the only remaining question for organized criminals is *what* they will do. This is where enterprise theory can contribute. These events can occur in any order, but it is important that a *how* (conspiracy), a *who* (ethnicity), and a *what* (illicit enterprise) come together to produce organized crime. The ethnic conspirators must decide what they are going to market: products or services, and to whom. They must determine if there is an existing demand for this product or service that is not being met, either in whole or in part, and can a demand be created or expanded. What is the competition? What is the territory? What are the risks, and how can they be controlled? Where will the capital investment come from? What about raw materials, supply, and distribution? What about supervision and management of employees? How will the profits be handled? Should they be laundered, reinvested, or invested in legitimate businesses? These are all decisions that must be made before carrying out a successful criminal enterprise. Some are single decisions; others are decisions that must be made again and again.

Whether a particular market is driven mainly by demand (reactive) or mainly by supply (proactive) not only has implications for the entrepreneurial emphasis, but also for control strategies. (The current drug market in the United States is an obvious example.) Other implications for control and prevention can be derived from enterprise issues such as:

- If the product/service being provided is illegal, might it be legalized? This would remove it from the realm of illicit enterprise; and, if the theory is correct, would eliminate it as a form of organized crime.
- If the product/service provided is legal, but in short supply, can the legal supply be expanded? This would take away the profit of illegal supply and again eliminate a form of organized crime.
- If the product/service is restricted, for example, licenses or other documentation, can the restrictions be revised or better enforced?
- Can demand be reduced through public education? "Just say no" is an example of this approach. If a product or service is no longer in demand, there will be no money to be made in providing it, and therefore another form of organized crime is eliminated.
- Can supply be reduced through control or elimination of necessary raw materials and distribution systems?
- Can risk be increased by attacking corruption?

These factors make it more costly to do business. Reducing the profit margin on any product or service reduces its attractiveness as a marketable commodity. On the other hand, as shown by criminal businesses such as human trafficking, increasing the risks for traffickers may backfire, by driving out the "amateurs," driving up the price (and the profit), and thus making the trafficking business more attractive for organized crime.

Rational choice, routine activities, and situational crime prevention

Membership in a criminal organization and engaging in organized crime involve a series of choices. For purposes of this last set of possible explanations of how this might work, let's divide the world of offenders into two broad categories: first, offenders whose criminal behavior is explained by *determinism*. Many of the approaches already discussed (cultural transmission, strain, ethnicity and ethnic succession) can be said to be deterministic – criminal behavior is "determined" by factors that are mostly outside the offender's control. Second is the category of offenders whose criminal behavior is explained by *free will*. The explanations and theories that underpin this rationale assume that criminals exercise free will in choosing to commit crimes; that they are rational actors. The set of explanations we will review next falls into this second category.

Rational choice theory

Rational choice theory (see Clarke & Cornish, 1986) assumes that offenders make reasoned decisions about committing crimes, after deciding that the chances of getting caught are relatively low, and the possibilities for a good pay-off are relatively high. It is a cost-benefit decision, in economic terms. Although rational choice theorists have largely focused on individual criminals committing individual crimes, it is not hard to imagine the members of a criminal organization together assessing the potential risks and benefits when considering whether to enter certain criminal markets, or, even earlier in the process, individuals deciding whether to form a criminal organization, join one, or remain involved in one, based on their weighing of the pluses and minuses.

The rational theorists' notion of rationality is not absolute; it is, rather, limited. Criminals may not calculate the costs and benefits accurately, may make foolish (in hindsight) choices, and may make decisions while affected by alcohol or drugs. Nevertheless, they are still making choices. We see these sorts of choices exercised in the elements of choice I have just described; how the crime is to be carried out (the conspiracy element), and what the crime will be (the illicit enterprise element). As I have emphasized, organized crime requires conspiracy; it also requires planning, and planning is also a rational process.

An example of how rational choice might describe and begin to explain a "crime that is organized," is found in the discussion of the international trafficking of stolen vehicles by Clarke and Brown (2003):

> All forms of trafficking in stolen cars involve a complex sequence of actions, including the following: preferred vehicles are identified and stolen, either to order or "on spec"; they may be moved to a safe place and their identities changed; they may be stored, awaiting pickup for transfer across the border; depending on the method of transfer, they may be placed in sealed containers and loaded onto ships, or they may be driven across the border. At the destinations, they may be handed over to a local contact or collected by such a person from the docks; they may be legally registered; and finally, they may be sold on the open market or to a private buyer ...

> The methods employed by traffickers, the routes they use, and the countries principally involved undergo constant change as a consequence of law enforcement activities or the changing opportunity structure for this crime ...

> ... Unraveling this complexity and gaining a detailed understanding of the phenomenon is a considerable challenge for researchers and policy makers alike.

> Clarke & Brown, (2003:206–207).

This certainly gives a sense of the planning behind, and the choices that have to be made in carrying out this crime. Examining these choices and their bases would provide valuable information to law enforcement officials and policy makers. Taking steps to increase the risks and reduce the benefits by "hardening the targets" of this crime would illustrate the predictive and control functions of rational choice theory.

Rational choice theory also has a heuristic value with respect to organized crime, as demonstrated in a study of the deterrent effect of enforcement operations on drug smuggling by Layne, et al., (2002). Mary Layne and her associates interviewed convicted and imprisoned high-level drug smugglers to find out how they balanced risk against reward in carrying out their crimes. Their conclusion was that, for these offenders, the calculation of risk was:

> ... hardly representative of a "criminal calculus" suggested by rational choice or deterrence theorists. Instead, risk was accepted as a given that had to be "neutralized" ... in order for the smuggling to take place ... A key element in the ability to neutralize ... risk was the magnitude of reward.

> Layne, et al., (2002:76).

The conclusion of the researchers, however, was very much that a criminal calculus took place. Concerns and doubts about the degree of risk were overcome, they said, by the "volume of reward that awaited them on the successful completion of a drug smuggling event:" the greater the perceived reward (benefit), the greater risk (potential cost) the smugglers were willing to accept. This sounds very much like a rational choice.

Sucker mentality

We might also think about rational choice operating in a slightly different fashion. One of the stumbling blocks for deterministic explanations is that people apparently experiencing essentially the same "determining" factors nevertheless make drastically different choices. Not all poor young Italian immigrants who came to the United States to live in the ghettos of New York City chose to drop out of school, join street gangs, or eventually get involved in the mafia. For some, crime was a choice, but for others it was not. What was (or is) the difference? Without over-simplifying a complex process, I think a "sucker mentality" is an important factor.

In a Social Darwinian world of the survival of the fittest, one of the routes to survival – working and studying – is difficult and often boring. Being straight – a "sucker" to some minds – requires self-discipline, sacrifice, and delayed gratification. It requires being at school or work, on time, perhaps early in the morning, all day, everyday. Running around until all hours is difficult, if not impossible, to combine with those obligations. Crime, on the other hand, has flexible hours. It is also exciting, dangerous and adventurous, and can produce greater and quicker pay-offs. Teenagers need only observe the difference between those (per-haps a parent) who rise early and spend long hours doing mind-numbing work for little pay, and those who sleep until noon then show up well-dressed, in snazzy cars, with good-looking girls on their arms. This is oversimplified, but nevertheless a perception that can influence rational choices.

It takes a conscious decision to step on the first rung of the crooked ladder, but like many other choices, the decision is shaped and constrained by a number of factors, such as "having an outlook that other people are suckers to be taken advantage of and that you are a sucker if you think you can get ahead by playing by the rules" (Finckenauer & Waring, 1998:37). Evidence, albeit limited, for this version of rational choice theory can be found in the work of Thomas Firestone (1993). Firestone examined thir-teen memoirs by Italian mobsters. He concluded that:

> ... none of the mobsters claims to have chosen crime because he was denied the opportunity to pursue a legitimate career. In fact,

> quite to the contrary, most of the authors indicate that they could
> have had legitimate careers, but simply preferred to be criminals.
>
> Firestone, (1993:202).

Having a mindset that "only saps work," may be an element of what the next theory categorizes as a "motivated offender."

Routine activities

The routine activities theory explains crime as being likely to occur when a motivated offender and a suitable victim (or crime target) come together in the absence of capable guardians (Cohen & Felson, 1979). Like the rational choice theory, it contains an assumption that offenders are rational actors who carefully pick their targets, based on factors such as accessibility, potential monetary yield, the expertise needed, and the time required to carry out the crime. The theory assumes that offenders also assess the risk of getting caught and the possible physical danger that might be involved in picking a suitable victim or target. Thus again, there is a weighing of potential costs and benefits.

The rational choice/routine activities approaches can readily be implemented in crime prevention policies. This is usually referred to as "situational crime prevention." These applications have, almost exclusively, been concerned with non-organized crimes. In one exception, Felson – one of the proposers of routine activities theory – relates how racketeering in the construction industry in New York City was characterized, by the New York State Organized Crime Task Force, as being a result of that industry being particularly susceptible to racketeering. In other words, construction was a suitable target because it created racketeering opportunities. According to Felson, by altering the structure of the construction industry, in accordance with situational crime prevention principles, organized crime could be made less likely (1998:178).

Crime opportunity theory

For another example, let us turn to the work of Jan J. M. van Dijk, formerly of the UN Center for International Crime Prevention. Van Dijk refers to the rational choice/routine activities approach as "crime opportunity theory" (not to be confused with the differential opportunity ideas associated with strain theory). In thinking about the relationship between organized crime, a country's rule of law, and its level of economic growth, van Dijk concludes that crime opportunity theory "helps to explain the extent and shape of transnational organized crime across countries." He observes that organized crime seems to be more prevalent in moderately poor rather than desperately poor countries, because the latter have fewer opportunities for the more lucrative crimes; for example, there is little demand in the poorest countries for illegal products, such as drugs. However, in moderately poor countries, pools of motivated offenders, who come from economically deprived groups, converge to exploit the criminal opportunities of the existing markets for illegal goods. If the laws, and the law enforcement and legal systems, are also corrupt and ineffective (that is, the rule of law is weak), this further facilitates the development of organized crime. Thus, says van Dijk, organized crime is most likely to be prevalent when all these conditions prevail.

Van Dijk acknowledges that the notion of crime resulting from a convergence of motivated offenders and criminal opportunities seems to fit less with organized than with common crime. Nevertheless, he believes that motivated offenders, viable criminal opportunities, and insufficient social control are all relevant factors for explaining organized crime rates. A country's existing criminal opportunities are more likely to be exploited by indigenous criminals from economically deprived groups.

However, global developments may mean that "favorable conditions for organized crime will increasingly also attract motivated offenders from abroad." Even if pools of motivated offenders in a country are restricted, says van Dijk, and opportunities for criminal gain are few, the low risk of discovery will attract foreign organized crime groups. Criminal activities may be shifted to the countries where the risks of detection, arrest, and/or confiscation of assets are the lowest. This illustrates the kind of costs/benefits weighing that the rational choice/routine activities theory assumes. Van Dijk believes that opportunities for organized crime will have an increasingly global appeal. Affluent countries, with no history of native organized crime can increasingly expect to be targeted by foreign criminal organizations. Van Dijk concludes:

> [T]he strength of informal and formal social controls may become the single most important determinant of the level of organized crime in individual countries. Where law enforcement, prosecution, the judiciary, and civil society are weak, both local and foreign groups will ruthlessly exploit existing or emerging opportunities for illegal gains.
>
> Jan J. M. van Dijk, "Does Crime Pay? On the Relationship Between Crime, Rule of Law and Economic Growth," *Forum on Crime and Society*, Vol. 1, No. 1, 2001, pp. 1–16.

Jay Albanese has also pursued the crime opportunity theory (Albanese, 2000; 2004). He argues that organized crime can be explained by three sets of factors: opportunity, criminal environment, and special access or skills. The opportunity factors, on which I shall primarily focus, are of four types: economic, governmental, law enforcement, and social and technological changes:

> Economic factors impact on the presence of organized crime through economic conditions such as poor standard of living, high demand for an illicit product or service combined with an affordable supply, and a competitive environment that makes it possible to cater to the demand.
>
> Albanese, (2004:23).

The governmental conditions and actions that can inhibit or contribute to organized crime include weak government, corruption, new laws, and regulations that create or expand criminal markets, such as taxation regimes, absence of money laundering prohibitions, and so on. Law enforcement factors refer to police resources and training, police corruption, and the politicizing of the police. Finally, social and technological developments, such as changes in the status of women, the ability to travel, access to the Internet, and cellphone coverage that "involve new individual freedoms or new technology can promote or limit opportunities for organized crime" (Albanese, 2004:26).

Knowledge of these crime opportunity factors, combined with knowledge about the nature of the potential offenders in the particular area and the capabilities and skills they have that enable them to exploit local crime opportunities, will, according to Albanese, enable us to predict the likely occurrence of organized crime. He has created a "Model of Criminal Opportunity-Organized Crime Group Interaction" (Albanese, 2000:416). Application of this model has demonstrated that the more predictive factors present in a particular environment, the higher the probability of widespread organized criminal activity (Albanese, 2000:421).

Why the mafia?

Putting aside the debate about the overuse of "mafia," there is considerable consensus among authorities on organized crime that the criminal organization that has dominated the Italian island of Sicily for hundreds of years is "a" mafia, and perhaps is the only "true" mafia (see, for example, Dickie, 2004). If a theory should enable us to explain a phenomenon, which theory explains the existence of the Sicilian Mafia? This complex and intriguing question has been considered by a number of mafia scholars and investigators, for example Arlacchi, Blok, Gambetta, Hess, Paoli, the

Schneiders, Stille, Dickie, and so on. I do not need, nor have I the space, to recount all their various views and conclusions but I recommend their writings to the reader who wishes to pursue this issue further.

The Sicilian Mafia represents a confluence of several elements; a unique set of circumstances that seems to account for this particular phenomenon. The first element is certain unique aspects of Sicilian culture. Sicilian culture, as described by the Schneiders (2003), is characterized by fatalism, and by exaggerated codes of honor and vendetta. Schneider and Schneider also point out, as does Diego Gambetta (1993), that Sicilians are "crippled by untrusting relations" and that because they are "chronically unable to trust each other, protection is genuinely needed and desired" (Schneider & Schneider, 2003:111). The second element is an economic environment that was, historically, ripe for exploitation: for example, the bidding process for public works' contracts, which had little or no governmental oversight or regulation and much corruption, was an attractive and vulnerable target for organized crime. Finally, politically weak, absent, and/or corrupt governmental authority, did not or could not exercise legal and political control on behalf of the people.

As Orlando, the former mayor of Palermo points out, the Sicilian people "never expected to receive justice from the 'system.' They looked to the charismatic *uomini di rispetto* (men of respect) to fulfill the functions that bureaucratic governments served everywhere else in Europe" (Orlando, 2001:11). The Sicilian people never really governed their own territory. As Orlando says, there was no middle class to care about and assume civic responsibilities, promote education, or own property and operate small businesses. The lower classes – the peasantry – that remained after the aristocracy fled, were weak, ignorant and vulnerable; easily cowed and perhaps submissive to mafia control. The Catholic Church, one of the most influential institutions in Sicilian society, also took a compliant stance.

Into this context strode the *gabelloti* and their successors, the mafioso. They were opportunistic and unscrupulous men; anxious (and able) to take criminal advantage of this vulnerable situation. Several of the explanations already offered would fit their identity and motivation, but of the selection of theories I have outlined, opportunity and rational choice theory perhaps best accounts for the rise, and continuance, of the Sicilian Mafia.

Peter Vitale's story, "Dining with a Godfather" (*Trends in Organized Crime*, Fall 2005) is a fascinating personal account of dealing with the Sicilian Mafia. Vitale concludes, among other things, that "[t]he naked fact is that the Mafia IS the government of Sicily" (Vitale, 2005:118).

The eclectic collection of explanations of organized crime I have reviewed in this chapter seems to fulfill the descriptive function: they all describe the circumstances in which an organized crime group can operate, and/or the necessary environment or conditions under which certain crimes can be committed; but they tell us less about the "motivated offender" who chooses to operate as a member of a criminal organization. The work of Albanese and van Dijk helps extend our understanding of how targets, offenders, and guardians can be related, with respect to organized crime. Future researchers will (and should) repeat and extend their work, thus fulfilling this heuristic function. Their work might enable us to apply the explanations and understanding to more effectively predict and control organized crime.

4
The many faces of organized crime

In the criminal world, there is no such thing as a dichotomy that divides crimes and criminals into "organized" and "everything else." I think it makes sense to array criminal organizations along a spectrum, according to how many of the attributes that characterize criminal organizations they have; attributes including sophistication, structure, stability, self-identification, and reputation. Crime groups that possess more of these attributes should be capable of wreaking more havoc on society.

Keeping this in mind, let us now look at a variety of criminal organizations. This will be an illustrative, rather than an exhaustive examination – a number of organizations is included, but many are not. The groups described represent, I believe, the major criminal organizations in the world. Some are indigenous to the United States, but most are either rooted elsewhere, or are transnational. This overview should shed more light on the distinction between the "mafia type" and other, more generic, forms of organized crime. I shall begin with the principal descendant of the Sicilian Mafia (which many consider to be the mother of all criminal organizations): *La Cosa Nostra*.

La Cosa Nostra

La Cosa Nostra (often commonly called the LCN, despite the redundancy of the "the") is the American version of the Italian mafia, whose roots can be traced to the 1800s. In 1890, the

Superintendent of Police of New Orleans, David Hennessey, was murdered. Chief Hennessey's killing was linked to gangs of Italian immigrants. Many (thousands) of the latter were alleged to have criminal records and to be linked to a secret criminal organization in Italy. Subsequent investigation and events refuted the wild allegations and conspiracy theories conjured around the Hennessey murder and the mafia's supposed role in it. Nevertheless, in the minds of many Americans, the concept of the "mafia," a worldwide secret criminal organization that was infiltrating the United States, stuck. As this belief became embedded in the American consciousness, the mafia myth began. (This is a clear example of the ethnic conspiracy theory described in the previous chapter.)

It is undeniable that, by the early 1900s and especially in New York City, a group of Italian-American organized crime "families" began operating. During the 1920s and 1930s, most especially after Prohibition, what was later called LCN became the most prominent collection of criminal organizations in the United States; the epitome of American organized crime. The most famous figures in the history of American organized crime were associated with LCN: Al Capone, Lucky Luciano, Frank Costello, Carlo Gambino, Vito Genovese, Joe Profaci, and more recently John Gotti and Vincent "Chin" Gigante.

LCN maintained its exalted criminal status for some fifty years until, beginning in the 1980s, they were severely crippled by a number of successful law enforcement efforts. During this period, the Italian-American families were also seriously challenged in a number of their criminal markets by other organized crime groups, such as Russians. Nevertheless, with respect to the criteria that best define the capacity of criminal organizations to cause harm, most authorities still regard LCN as a dangerous threat to American society, because it has a greater capacity than any of its competitors to gain monopoly control over criminal markets, to use or threaten violence to maintain that control, and to corrupt the law enforcement and political systems. This particular

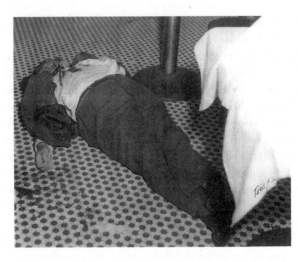

Figure 4 Willie Moretti, the supposed Mafia boss of New Jersey, was a member of the Genovese LCN crime family. Moretti was shot to death on October 4, 1951 – allegedly because he had a "loose lip" – by hitmen who had taken him to lunch.

capacity distinguishes LCN from most other criminal organizations in the US.

Nationwide, the estimated "made membership" (males of Italian descent) of LCN is over one thousand, roughly eighty per cent of whom operate in New York City and metropolitan New Jersey. Five crime families make up LCN in the New York area: the Bonanno, Colombo, Genovese, Gambino, and Lucchese families. There is also a lesser LCN presence in Boston, Chicago, Philadelphia, and the Miami\South Florida area. As well as the made members, an estimated ten thousand associate members work for the families. They are not made members, because they may not be of Italian descent, because the "books are closed" in a particular family, because they do not have a sponsor who regards them as worthy of membership, or perhaps simply because they do not choose to be made.

The origins of LCN in the Sicilian Mafia and other Italian organized crime groups (like the *Camorra* or *'Ndrangheta*) are evident in the initiation into and codes for membership. Initiation is achieved in a secret, ritualized induction ceremony. Made members are usually called "wiseguys" or "goodfellas." Made membership means both honor and increased income, but also entails responsibilities – in particular, the taking the oath of *omerta*. Omerta demands silence toward the outside world about the criminal affairs of the family, never betraying anyone in the family, and never revealing to law enforcement officers anything that might incriminate anyone in organized crime. The penalty for violating the oath is supposed to be death. However, there are hundreds of members of LCN who, for assisting in government prosecutions of their fellow mobsters, are under the US Federal Witness Protection program – which suggests that *omerta* is not nearly as effective as it perhaps once was. This same phenomenon has occurred in Italy, where the turncoats are called *pentiti* (the penitent ones).

LCN established its reputation for the ruthless use of violence over many years. More than most other criminal organizations, LCN typifies the systematic use of violence as a business method. Violence – or the threat of violence – has been the means by which LCN gained monopoly control over its criminal enterprises. Violence discouraged and eliminated competitors and reinforced LCN's reputation and credibility. Violence was, and is, used for internal discipline. The history of violence and LCN demonstrates the importance of reputation (see Reuter, 1994). When there is sufficient credible evidence of a mob's willingness to use violence, actual violence is rarely necessary. *La Cosa Nostra* personifies this principle.

La Cosa Nostra's illegal activities are wide-ranging; gambling and drugs have traditionally been their biggest money makers. Loan sharking, often linked with the gambling and drugs, is an activity that exemplifies the role played by violence. The same is true of extortion. More traditional crimes include hijacking, air cargo theft, and murder. The specialties of the five New York families also include labor racketeering, various kinds of business racketeering, bid-rigging, business fraud, and industry cartels. In its penetration and "governing" of these legitimate industries, LCN most resembles the traditional Sicilian mafia, albeit in a limited sense.

Partly as a result of effective law enforcement actions in many of its traditional areas in recent years, La Cosa Nostra has diversified its activities and extended its infiltration of legal markets, switching to white-collar type crimes (Raab, 1997). LCN has carried out multi-million dollar frauds in three areas: health insurance, pre-paid telephone cards, and the victimizing of small Wall Street brokerage houses. La Cosa Nostra's monopoly control over various illegal markets, and its diversification into legal markets, has not so far been matched by any other criminal organization in the United States.

La Cosa Nostra is a cause for concern for the FBI and law enforcement agencies in New York City. Elsewhere in the US, it is low priority, with the attention paid to it characterized by experts as "hit and miss," because of a belief that "things are under control." La Cosa Nostra is mainly a domestic operation, and because the FBI's priorities now center on combating terrorism, there is little emphasis on international cooperation in the investigation and prosecution of LCN.

Urban street gangs

Anyone who pays even the most casual attention to the news will be familiar with the nature and magnitude of a problem that is both old and new – street gangs, particularly urban street gangs. In the United States, such gangs are as old as the end of the American Revolution, like the gangs portrayed in Gangs of New York, Martin

Scorsese's 2002 movie about the history of gangs in New York City. American gangs evolved into the Chicago gangs studied by Thrasher (1927) in the 1920s, and on to those portrayed in the 1950s play and film *West Side Story*.

But street gangs are a worldwide problem. In South Africa, the Soweto Bo-Tsotsi (youth gangs) have dominated the Soweto township area for generations (Glaser, 2000). Tsotsi gang members, hundreds of them, reject work and the law, and esteem violence and drugs. According to Clive Glaser, a combination of social and economic deprivation, and the consequent adoption of their own sub-culture, has led these super-violent gangs to robbery, gambling, bootlegging, prostitution, murder, assault, and rape.

Street gangs are very much a current and continuing problem. They carry out their violence on the streets of many cities, often using modern weapons, such as assault rifles and grenades. The gangs, which receive much media (and law enforcement) attention are often involved in varied criminality and certainly appear to be organized. Reports from researchers and law enforcement experts indicate that many gangs have evolved into new, often very violent, forms. In some areas, for example the State of New Jersey, such gangs are now the most serious organized crime problem. The new "super gangs" are more similar in structure and criminal activity to traditional organized crime groups than to the *relatively* harmless collections of teenagers who made up the more typical street gangs of the past.

The exemplars of the most dangerous and deadly gangs are the Bloods, the Crips, and the Almighty Latin Kings and Queens, which have existed for a number of years. Of more recent vintage, are the Neta, the Mara Salvatrucha or MS–13, and the Mara 18 or Los Angeles 18th Street gang. The Latin Kings originated on the streets of Chicago, and the Neta in the prisons of Puerto Rico. Los Angeles, the "world capital of street gangs," is the birthplace of the others. The Bloods originated in South Central Los Angeles in the late 1960s. They are a primarily African-American gang, with both male and female members. They have chapters, and many thousands of members, across the United States, mostly in urban areas; their principal criminal activity is drug distribution. The Crips were also formed in South Central Los Angeles in 1969–70, and they too have spread nationwide. Also primarily African-American, and with both male and female members, the Crips are the Bloods' bitter rivals. They have gained a reputation for being particularly dangerous and violent. The convicted killer Stanley "Tookie' Williams, executed at San Quentin prison in December 2005, was a co-founder of the Crips gang.

Both the Bloods and the Crips use extreme violence to protect their drug sales' "turf" and to discourage competition. This violence is sometimes directed at each other, at other gangs and rival organized crime groups, and sometimes at innocent bystanders. Gang members give prison administrators enormous headaches whenever they are imprisoned.

The Latino gangs – Mara Salvatrucha and Mara 18 – represent a new threat in the street gang menace. Since in the 1990s, these gangs, and others like them have spread from the United States across Central America and Mexico. These groups, with an estimated membership close to 100,000, have killed thousands of people. These Latino super-gangs are sophisticated, highly structured, self-identified as gang members, and with a formidable reputation. Law enforcement sources describe their structures as elaborate and flexible, with both a leadership group and a backup. They have strong self-identification, with elaborate internal rules, unique tattoos, and their own language – both signed and written. They use cell phones, and the internet and have their own web pages. Finally, their capacity for, use of, and reputation for violence are so great that in certain areas in El Salvador and Guatemala the maras are said to be acting as surrogate or alternate governments. They levy taxes and kill those who don't pay. The "official" government more-or-less leaves them alone, because the police lack the capacity to deal with them (Bruneau, 2005).

THE MARAS AND NATIONAL SECURITY IN CENTRAL AMERICA

... In the context of the [1980s] wars and insurgencies in El Salvador, Guatemala, and Nicaragua, thousands of people, including young men, fled North, a great many arriving as illegal aliens in Los Angeles, California. A certain percentage of these young men had been involved in the conflict, either on the side of the governments or the insurgents, and were familiar with guns and armed combat. In Los Angeles they encountered a difficult work and social situation, which was already structured in terms of gangs involving, in particular, African Americans in the Crips and Bloods, Mexican-Americans, and illegal Mexican immigrants in the EME or Mexican Mafia. A certain percentage of these young men, especially those from El Salvador ... joined the 18th Street Gang ... [Other] Salvadorans founded the Mara Salvatrucha, to compete with the former, considering the Salvadorans in M-18 traitors ...

[Since] most of the maras were involved in criminal activity, they were arrested and put into prison. In prison they further defined and honed their gang identities and criminal skills. With the peace processes ending the war in El Salvador in 1992, and spreading throughout the region by the mid-1990s, the US Government deported the maras on [their] release from prison back to their countries of origin ... Once back in San Salvador, Guatemala City, San Pedro Sula, etc. the maras established themselves in these war-torn societies, and have been growing ever since.

Mara Salvatrucha, or MS-13, already fully formed in Los Angeles, was established in San Salvador in 1992 by the clicas (cliques) deported from the United States and replaced earlier, less violent, and less sophisticated gangs. M-18 was established in El Salvador in 1996 with three clicas ...

In El Salvador there are approximately 11,000 active members divided among MS-13 (7,000), M-18 (4,000), and others (200) ... [T]he [estimated] membership numbers for all the countries in the region are as follows: Honduras (36,000 in 112 groups); Guatemala (14,000 in 434 groups); El Salvador (11,000 in 4); Nicaragua (4,500 in 268);

THE MARAS AND ... AMERICA (*contd.*)

Costa Rica (2,700 in 6); Panama (1,400 in 94); and Belize (100 in 2 groups), for a regional total of 69,145 in 920 groups.*

The Maras are not only a Central America regional phenomenon; rather they are transnational. The MS-13, for example, reportedly has 20,000 members in the United States and 4,000 members in Canada, for a total of 96,000 in the hemisphere ...

... [T]he [Civilian National Police] in El Salvador list the following [criminal] activities ... for the Maras: selling drugs; extortion; prostitution; homicide; and illegal movement of drugs, people, and arms across borders ... [T]he two major sources of income are the drug trade and extortions ... They can function as networks, with extensive transnational linkages ... They increasingly arm their members ... with heavier weapons including M-16s, AK-47s, and grenades. Their members are reported to be increasingly sophisticated in using these arms.

*These data are from the Civilian National Police in El Salvador.

Thomas C. Bruneau, Strategic Insights, Volume IV, Issue 5 (May 2005)

Although there is disagreement on what constitutes a "gang," the term generally describes a group of adolescents or young adults who share an identity and neighborhood, use common symbols, and "may sometimes engage in illegal activities" (Johnson & Muhlhausen, 2005:39). The super-gangs, a subset of the general gang category, are obviously at the high end of the "engaging in illegal activities" scale. Thus, they share certain characteristics with other recognized criminal organizations such as LCN. Those characteristics include similarities in leadership structures, a clear division of labor, purposefulness in making of money through illicit means, networks of members across cities, specialization in certain types of criminal activity such as drug trafficking, the use of clandestine initiation rituals to induct new members, and the use of written or formalized rules of conduct that guide the activities of their members. However, criminal enterprise is not usually the gangs' main goal (unlike traditional organized crime), corruption is not used extensively, if at all, and the use of violence is not instrumental for achieving legitimacy but is usually impulsive and gratuitous. Urban street gangs provide an alternative form of social grouping for their young members; a system within which young men can gain psychological rewards and status. Young people who have been rejected – or who at least perceive that they have been rejected – gain acceptance by joining a gang. Whether these gangs are a form of organized crime is debatable; experts are divided on the issue. The super-gangs certainly come close to meeting the definition. But they are not a mafia.

Outlaw Motorcycle Gangs/One percent biker clubs

Outlaw motorcycle gangs (OMG) came into being in the United States during the period following World War II, when groups of young men, many newly-returned war veterans, formed motor- cycle clubs and rejected normal civilian life. Recalling the earlier discussion of some of the theories put forward to explain orga- nized crime, theories such as cultural conflict and strain seem particularly applicable to how and why OMG arose. A sense of alienation, of economic and social frustration, and *anomie* or lack of values characterized (and still characterizes) the lower class white men who came together to form these gangs. These factors were especially prevalent among returning Vietnam veterans in the 1970s. A similar phenomenon occurred in the former Soviet Union when that country's veterans of the 1980s war in Afghanistan (the "Afghansty") returned home similarly disaffected and disillusioned.

As happened with the Italian-American mafia, during the 1950s and 1960s a mythology developed around motorcycle

Figure 1 Members of the "The Breed" outlaw motorcycle gang – a local gang in the United States. The Breed uses violence to settle disputes and enforce policy, and has exerted considerable influence in the drug market.

riders and motorcycle clubs, promulgated by such films as *The Wild Ones, Easy Rider,* and *Angels on Wheels.* Marlon Brando and Peter Fonda personified rebellion, freedom to do your own thing, and being anti-establishment. This perception of motorcycle gangs has changed since then; "outlaw" motorcyclists have become much less romantic figures and are today more likely to be viewed as common criminals, or worse.

The "one percenter" self-identification derives from an American Motorcycle Association estimate, made some years ago, that outlaw motorcyclists made up less than one per cent of the motorcyclists. It is estimated that there are around three hundred one percent biker clubs in the United States (See www.nagia.org/NGTASection_II.htm). The largest have members in many other countries. They engage in a multitude of crimes, including murder, extortion, kidnapping, arson, robbery, bombings, receiving stolen property, drug manufacture, and drug trafficking. Producing and dealing synthetic drugs such as methamphetamine is their principal source of income. Some gangs have ties to street gangs, drug cartels, and to LCN. They often provide muscle, firearms, bombs, or drugs for the Italian mob.

The "Big Four" OMG or biker clubs have gained national and international stature as the most notorious and radical of the mold: the Hells Angels, the Outlaws, the Pagans, and the Bandidos. They are recognized as the largest and most powerful of the OMG because of their membership and degree of criminal involvement. Together, they are estimated to have a worldwide membership of over 10,000 (though the Pagans are not believed to have any international chapters (Barker, 2005)). Australia, Canada, Europe, and the Scandinavian countries have chapters of the other three clubs; but so too do Liechtenstein (Hells Angels), the Channel Islands and Luxemborg (Bandidos), and Thailand (Outlaws).

OMG generally adhere to a particular philosophy, and stress initiation rituals, the wearing of colors, codes of conduct, and rules of secrecy. Biker philosophy includes striving to live lives totally unlike those of others in the community. They do not want to live as normal citizens; therefore, they reject generally accepted norms and adopt their own morals, ethics and values, reflected in their dress, mannerisms, and criminal lifestyle – much of which the rest of society considers repellent, offensive, shocking, and disgusting. The outlaw motorcycle gangs, especially the Big Four, espouse a philosophy that incorporates the reliance on violence and discipline characteristic of organized crime: for example, the charters and rules for the gangs spell out the penalties for breaking the rules, including the burning off of club tattoos and assassination.

OMG share a propensity for instrumental violence and a willingness to use corruption with more traditional organized crime groups. They use violence as a means of controlling competition and enforcing internal discipline, and corruption as a method of preventing detection, arrest and prosecution. The Big Four also display a continuity and sophistication in their criminal operations.

OMG have an organized hierarchy, sophisticated operations, and internal discipline and bonding. They are extremely violent; they have many criminal enterprises, providing illegal goods and services such as drugs, prostitution, gambling, and guns and other weapons; they corrupt the police and perhaps other public officials to immunize themselves from law enforcement; and they invest their ill-gotten profits in a host of legitimate businesses. They would certainly seem to be a true form of organized crime.

The Russian "Mafiya"

Organized crime has a history over four hundred years' long in Russia – a history marked by blurred distinctions between the legal and illegal and the public and private, and a very feeble commitment to the rule-of-law. This means, among other things, that Russian organized crime is not peculiar to the Soviet era, although it certainly metastasized during the seventy-five years of Soviet rule. For example, the *vorovskoi mir* (thieves' world), a criminal subculture of pre-Soviet times, evolved into an elite group of criminals – the *vory v zakone* (thieves-in-law). Many *vory* were imprisoned in Joseph Stalin's *gulags* between 1929 and 1953. After Stalin's death in 1953, many of these *vory*, as well as other lesser criminals, were freed. The freed *vory* colonized the rest of the criminal underworld to become partners in a three-tiered system of organized crime in Soviet Russia that operated until the collapse of the USSR in 1991.

This criminal pyramid had a broad foundation of professional criminals, including *vory*. Above this were the "shadow economy" and black-market operators. These factory and farm workers and directors produced goods and products "off the books," that is, outside the state-imposed quota. Others used their positions in hotels or work involving foreign travel to purchase, for resale, unavailable or illegal goods and products. The shadow economy

Figure 6 Vyacheslav "Yaponchik" Ivankov, allegedly a top boss of the Russian mafia, had a long criminal record in the former Soviet Union. He was arrested in 1995 and convicted for trying to extort $3.5 million from a Russian-owned business (AP Photo/Monika Graff).

surplus and black-market items were then sold outside official channels, with pay-offs to government and Communist Party officials. These high-level government and Communist Party bureaucrats, the *apparatchiks* and *nomenklatura*, sat at the top of the pyramid, skillfully exploiting the system to line their own pockets.

Among the things that are important about this history is first, the unusual inter-relationship (symbiosis) between crime – especially organized crime – and economic and political structures. This symbiosis very much persists in Russia today. Second, given that most goods and services were in chronically short supply in the USSR, the concept or practice of *blat* (using connections and informal networks) to get access to those goods and services became very important. Connected with this was the development, to a very high degree, of a "connive to survive" mentality.

The emphasis on, and highly adept use of, *blat* and conniving are today still very much evident, both at home and abroad, in the kind of crimes at which Russians, as well as others from the former Soviet Union, are especially skilled. This is illustrative of the "sucker mentality" that I described earlier and is one way of explaining why certain individuals make a rational choice to engage in the sorts of crimes that require guile and deceit.

In Russia today, organized crime has deeply penetrated business and economic enterprises. The *krysha* (roof) protection system means that many businesses are the victims of extortion and protection rackets. The rapid privatization of former state-held businesses enabled organized crime to capture many key economic assets. The collapse of security opened the door to widespread theft; in particular, to the theft and sale of military arms and equipment. Corruption has been facilitated, the legal and political systems have been infiltrated, legitimate private business has been discouraged, the rule-of-law has been undermined, and the development of civil society has been retarded. Overseas, mostly in the United States, the UK, Australia, Canada and Israel, the so-called "Russian Mafiya" (although it is not a mafia in the literal sense) presents two types of threat. Loosely structured networks of criminal entrepreneurs from the former Soviet Union engage in various deceits – white-collar crimes such as health care and insurance frauds, counterfeiting, stock and bank frauds, and so on. The bootlegged gasoline scheme, to evade gasoline taxes in the US, is an example of this type of crime; this particular criminal enterprise was operated in a union with some LCN families in the New York metropolitan area. The individuals involved are usually not affiliated with any known Russian criminal organizations, and they may or may not have any prior criminal background. Their crimes are organized, but are not organized crime.

The second international threat comes from affiliates or cells of known organized crime groups in Russia, for example, the *Solntsevskaya* and *Ismailovskaya*, which are involved in a wide array

DRUG SPREAD IN RUSSIA THREATENS NATIONAL SECURITY

The spread of drugs in Russia over the past decade has come to pose a threat to the health of the country's population and [to the] national security as a whole ...

The Russian Federation has become the object of an active expansion on the part of international drug traffickers. Over half of all the drugs discovered come to Russia from abroad: in 2002 the customs services confiscated 9 tons of drugs. More than 3,000 people from 34 different countries were arrested for drug trafficking in Russia in 2002. According to the Russian Interior Ministry ... the main drug importer to Russia is Afghanistan.

Recently, this international drug crime has been increasingly spreading across Russia. New channels for importing synthetic drugs have been detected in the Baltic states. All the drug gangs operating in Russia are said to be ethnicity-based, with the largest of them being Gypsies and Tajiks.

There is also an obvious and rather dangerous interaction between drug trafficking and extremism and terrorism. The profits from drugs sales are used to sponsor terrorist groups, to destabilize the political situation, and/or to stir up regional conflicts.

Organized Crime Study Center, Vladivostok, Russia (2005)

of traditional organized crime activities in the former Soviet Union, including drugs, human trafficking, arms trafficking, stolen vehicles, and so on. In particular, criminal gangs are moving drugs, including cocaine, from Afghanistan through Russia and on to Europe.

The illicit proceeds of this potpourri of criminal activities are, typically, laundered through, US or British financial institutions. The gangs also help corrupt businessmen and politicians to move financial assets out of Russia. Bank fraud and international money laundering are a significant threat to a number of countries;

because of globalization and the collapse of border controls, Russian criminal organizations find it relatively easy to travel and to mount transnational criminal operations. Some of their crimes, such as cybercrime and money laundering, do not actually require travel.

The pervasiveness of Russian organized crime is, to a great extent, a product of the history and traditions I described earlier; also, there is currently a ready availability and presence of violent entrepreneurs or predatory men (Volkov, 2002). These entrepreneurs of violence include former military or security personnel (often well-educated and relatively sophisticated) who have lost their jobs, sportsmen whose clubs and activities are no longer being subsidized by the government, or they are newly-released prisoners. Together, they represent a pool of potential criminals, ready to conspire and work with professional criminals like the *vory*, and with the shady businessmen and corrupt politicians who so dominate the Russian scene.

The violent entrepreneurs, as well as others, are motivated because of the shortfall between their aspirations and expectations and the reality of life in today's Russia, while the "haves" who are simply trying to have more seem mostly to be motivated by greed for money and power. The disillusion of young men in the first group is true also of the young Russian women who fall victim to smuggling or trafficking and end up working in the sex industries in Europe, China, Japan, Taiwan, Australia, Israel, or the United States. The situation in Russia, and elsewhere in the former Soviet Union, very much resembles the "fertile environment" for the growth of crime, as described by the criminal opportunity theories. There are numerous vulnerabilities to be exploited, the security system protecting potential targets has collapsed or been corrupted, and there are many disaffected young males – or plain predators – ready to take advantage of those opportunities and attack those targets.

The Japanese *yakuza*

Yakuza is the collective name for a number of different crime groups operating within and without Japan. *Yakuza* refers to a losing hand in a card game, and is believed to come from one of this criminal organization's antecedents, the *bakuto* or gamblers (Hill, 2005). Gambling, and other mostly non-violent crimes, such as drug dealing, are the stock-in-trade of some of the groups that comprise the *yakuza*. Also within *yakuza* are the *boryokudan* (violent ones) groups, regarded as the most dangerous and serious threat, because of their pathological use of violence. Japanese police statistics for 2002 estimated *boryokudan* membership to be about 85,000 (Hill, 2005), which contrasts with an earlier (1963) estimate of roughly 185,000. The decline is attributed to a combination of more aggressive policing, new laws, changing economic conditions, and to changes in police data collection procedures.

The largest *boryokudan* group is the Yamaguchi-Gumi, which has an estimated 39,000 members (The Japan Times, August 19, 2005). "Yamaguchi-Gumi is a large, hierarchically structured group engaged in a wide range of criminal activities" (UN Global Studies on Organized Crime, 2000:130), including activities outside Japan and sometimes in coordination with other organized crime groups. Their crimes include activities typically associated with organized crime: drug trafficking, extortion, gambling, prostitution, money laundering, armed robbery, trafficking in stolen goods and firearms, kidnapping for ransom, and insurance fraud. Recently, the *yakuza* have engineered internet frauds in which spurious or excessive charges are levied on visitors to pornographic and other sites (Hill, 2005).

According to Hill (2005), criminal activities overseas by *yakuza* affiliates include extortion from Japanese companies working outside Japan, operating clubs, bars, and sex industry establishments that cater for Japanese businessmen overseas, smuggling illegal workers, drugs and arms into Japan and investing in foreign real estate. They are notably present in Australia, the United States (Hawaii and California), and throughout Asia. Some *boryokudan* crimes are carried out in cooperation with other criminal organizations: for example, the heroin and methamphetamine brought into Japan is supplied by Chinese organized groups in Taiwan and Hong Kong, and cocaine comes via Latin American drug traffickers. Arms are obtained from Chinese and Russian organized crime groups and from the United States.

Japanese organized criminal groups also engage in legal enterprises, such as the entertainment business, real estate, and construction. But even in those areas, ostensibly "legal" businesses can cover criminal activity. For example, "entertainment" can include operating brothels, massage parlors and pornography outlets, Japanese criminals have been major players in organizing the sexual slavery of women from China, Southeast Asia, Russia, and the Philippines; real estate can be a cover for money laundering, and construction can include rigging bids for contracts and using violence against potential competitors.

Traditionally, *boryokudan* have distinctive group structures, behavior patterns, codes, values, and jargon. They have been highly structured, based on hierarchical systems of elder and younger brothers in a feudal-paternal family structure, though this "father-son" pattern is now said to be waning. Recruitment is mostly from educational dropouts and low achievers, and specifically from juvenile street gangs and biker gangs (Uchiyama, 2003:273). In the past, great emphasis was placed on ritual, including ceremonial initiations (involving rice, fish, salt, and sake), body tattooing, and self-mutilation by finger-cutting. A member who angered a supervisor would apologize by amputating a finger or finger joint and presenting it to the offended supervisor. Although still practiced, all these rituals are less rigidly adhered to now.

Historically closely associated with business interests and with political figures at the highest levels of the government, *boryokudan* connections were particularly evident in post-World War II

Japan. In the aftermath of the war, *boryokudan* became involved in the black market of untaxed goods, and then moved into the entertainment and gambling businesses and the drug trade. *Boryokudan* enforcers, sometimes employing violence, are still used in Japan to maintain order at stockholder meetings.

The *boryokudan* once enjoyed a degree of acceptance in Japan, not only among businessmen and politicians, but also among the general public, because they were seen as a "self-defense people's army against aggressors and looters" (UN Global Studies on Organized Crime, September 2000:36). However, this acceptance is said to have changed, to such an extent that "they are now regarded as anti-social organizations that are vigorously opposed by public agencies and community activists" (UN Global Studies, 2000:131). Their social acceptance, even if it may now be lessening, is unlike the situation of most other criminal organizations in most other countries in the world, with the possible exception of the Sicilian Mafia and groups which operate in Russian cities like Ekaterinburg and Vladivostok, where they have thoroughly infiltrated the business and political establishments. No similar level of acceptance has ever been attained by *La Cosa Nostra* in the United States. *Yakuza* also have an ultra-nationalistic, conservative, and anti-communist political orientation that makes them much more ideological than most criminal organizations.

The *boryokudan* are obviously very sophisticated, highly structured, well-disciplined, and complex criminal organizations that use violence, corruption, diverse activities, money laundering, and infiltration of legitimate businesses to carry out a broad array of licit and illicit enterprises. Theirs is, unquestionably, organized crime on an international scale. As to mafia-like characteristics, the *boryokudan* have engaged in "crisis management" (which typically means resolving personal or business disputes outside court), as well as a "security" function – thus taking on a quasi-governmental role. However, these particular kinds of functions appear to be diminishing today.

Chinese "Mafia"

The umbrella terms "Chinese organized crime" and "Chinese Mafia" cover a wide variety of entities, including secret societies and triads, organized criminal gangs, "mafia-like" underworld groups, tongs, street gangs, and human smuggling, human trafficking, and drug trafficking networks. All are criminal organizations; some purely domestic with local operations, others transnational and still others indigenous to Chinese immigrant communities in other countries. Among the most commonly known of these organizations are the triads, the tongs and the street gangs.

"Triads" are secret societies, originally formed in China in the early seventeenth century, in resistance to the Ching Dynasty. They are patriotic and nationalistic; formed originally as religious, peasant rebellion, or political groups. Triads are especially seen in Hong Kong and Macau – former European colonies that are now special administrative districts of China. According to Chin (1986), among the most criminally sophisticated are the Hong Kong–based 14 K and Wo Shing Wo groups. Some academic and legal authorities consider the origin, evolution, rituals, and practices of the triads to be very similar to those of the Sicilian Mafia (Keene, 1989).

"Tong" refers to a hall or gathering place. The tongs function as benevolent associations, business associations, ethnic societies, and centers of local politics. They engage in political and protest activities (emanating from the fact that they are rather alienated from more legitimate organizations) and sometimes criminal activities. They may be fronts or covers for Chinese street gangs, enabling them to prey on Chinese immigrants and Chinese business owners in the Chinatowns of western cities. Whereas the tongs are involved in illegal gambling, their affiliates engage in crimes such as extortion, drug trafficking, robbery, and protection schemes for prostitution and pornography businesses.

Chinese street gangs are a special case of urban street gangs; a feature of city Chinatowns settled by Chinese immigrants. They were originally affiliated with their tong overseers, and acted as para-professional criminal organizations, guarding the gambling dens run by the tongs. But in the mid-1970s, especially in New York City, well-armed gang members became so powerful that the tongs could no longer control them. "When the street youths emerged as powerful street gangs through the financial and moral support of the tongs, the gangs overran the tongs and indulged in their own criminal activities such as extortion, robbery, and murder" (Chin, 1986: 279). Chin indicates that the gangs are exclusively male, aged between thirteen and thirty-seven, and mostly immigrants from Hong Kong or China. Their crimes include protection rackets, extortion of legitimate Chinese-owned businesses, robbery of exclusively Chinese victims, prostitution run from massage parlors, drug trafficking, and gang warfare.

With this as introduction, let us turn to the current situation in China, Taiwan, and Hong Kong. This discussion of "Chinese organized crime" or "Chinese mafia" is based on a report made by Ko-lin Chin and me, from a study for the US Department of Justice in 2003–04 (see Finckenauer and Chin, 2004).

China

Our interviews with mainland Chinese authorities and academics made it clear that, in their view, the most serious organized crime problems facing China are (in order of seriousness): drug distribution, gambling, prostitution, and violence. The Chinese government is alarmed by the dramatic increase in the number of heroin addicts, and believes that local and foreign drug syndicates are responsible for importing heroin from the neighboring Golden Triangle of Southeast Asia and distributing it throughout China. Gambling and prostitution were believed to have been wiped out by the Chinese Communists following the Communist takeover in 1949, but have returned to China with a vengeance. As crime groups are becoming better-armed and more violent, the Chinese authorities are increasingly concerned about the violent acts committed by mobsters against rival gang members, ordinary citizens, business owners, and government authorities.

In an interview, a senior investigator from the Criminal Investigation Division of the Ministry of Public Security in Beijing, said:

> Our main concerns are: (1) organizations having an underworld nature (or what is referred to as a mafia-like character) that will penetrate into the legitimate business sector; (2) gangsters who will get involved in politics and run for public office; and (3) eventual hook-ups between these gangsters and foreign-based organized crime groups.

There is already evidence to suggest that crime groups in China have monopolized wholesale businesses and that the majority of these groups are protected by local authorities under the *baohusan*, or "protecting umbrella" – in other words, bribery and corruption. Official corruption is seen as a significant and growing problem, as exemplified by the syndicates and "Black Societies" of China.

Both the investigator to whom we spoke, and others, stressed that organized crime is largely a regional or urban phenomenon in China, rather than a national or transnational phenomenon. Given the pace of economic development in China, and the interest of external investors in its development, this extensive involvement of criminal organizations has significant implications, including a potentially chilling effect on China's future economic growth.

Tens of thousands of Chinese men and women are smuggled abroad every year, and the large numbers of undocumented Chinese laborers and sex workers are a major concern in many countries (See Smith 1997, Kwong 1997, Emerton 2001, Brazil

THE LIANG XIAO MIN SYNDICATE

In 1993, Liang Xiao Min, a policeman in the Public Security Bureau of Chang Chin (in northeastern China) established a syndicate of some dozen local supporters and three police colleagues. By 1994, the syndicate had expanded to more than twenty members, armed with illegal guns. In fewer than seven years, the syndicate purchased or opened several businesses, including casinos, nightclubs, sauna baths, fast food restaurants, and garages. The businesses were all legitimately registered, but some were used as covers for underground gambling houses and prostitution. Liang utilized his position as a police officer to finance his growing commercial interests; forcing banks to grant him loans through violence and intimidation. (When a bank manager refused to loan Liang US $220,000, his men attacked her and broke her leg.) Liang boasted:

> I have three magic weapons: First, I am a policeman. Who is not afraid of me? Second, I am the head of a "Black Society" syndicate. Who dares to offend me? Third, I have connections to the people with power. Who can do anything about me?

Liang called his syndicate a "family," set up "house rules," and headed the "household." When, in 2000, the Liang Xiao Min Syndicate was brought to trial, it was one of the largest "Black Society" groups ever brought to justice in China. Thirty-five members were convicted of serious crimes; seven members were sentenced to death and the remainder to various terms of imprisonment

Trends in Organized Crime, Vol.6, No. 2 Winter 2000, pp. 134–135

2004). However, the Chinese authorities consider this neither as a major problem nor one of organized crime. Some Chinese officials claim that this is not specifically a "Chinese problem," because most of the human smugglers are Chinese-Americans (Chin 1999). Local authorities point out the many benefits of a large number of people working abroad and sending money home. Indeed, we observed a considerable number of new housing developments outside the city of Fuzhou; developments fueled by money allegedly sent home by illegal workers in the United States.

Taiwan

In Taiwan, the major organized crime problem is *heijin*; the penetration of mobsters into the legitimate business sector and political arena (Chin 2003). Influential gangsters are now the CEOs of major business conglomerates, heavily involved in the businesses of bid-rigging, waste disposal, construction, cable television, telecommunications, stock trading, and entertainment. Since the mid-1980s, many criminals, to protect themselves from police crackdowns, have sought public office as a way to gain the immunity associated with office-holding. It is estimated that, today, some one-third of the elected deputies in Taiwan are current or former gangsters.

As well as *heijin*, the Taiwanese authorities are concerned with "traditional" organized crime activities: gambling, prostitution, loan sharking, debt-collection, extortion, and gang violence. Kidnapping for ransom is also a major concern, because influential and wealthy figures are often targeted and, as a result, a large number of Taiwanese entrepreneurs have left Taiwan for safe haven abroad. A relatively recent, but growing, crime problem, transnational in nature, is the production and distribution of pirated CDs and DVDs. The three major criminal gangs active in Taiwan are said to be involved in this business.

Even though Taiwan is a destination country for heroin from the Golden Triangle and amphetamines from China, Taiwanese authorities are more concerned with the influx of Chinese sex workers (or potential sex workers). These sex workers are smuggled (or trafficked) into Taiwan by boats across the Taiwan Strait or through fraudulent marriages with Taiwanese citizens. A midnight police raid of a sex club (not in itself illegal) in Taipai, which we were invited to observe, was to determine whether illegal Chinese women were working there. Over one thousand young

Chinese women, some detained for more than nine months, were awaiting deportation back to mainland China from a detention facility we visited. The Taiwanese law enforcement personnel we interviewed were frustrated in dealing with the human smuggling issue because the Chinese authorities are not cooperative, and because judges in Taiwan are reluctant to apply the country's anti-organized crime laws to human trafficking networks. The judges apparently do not regard human smuggling and trafficking as an organized crime problem.

Hong Kong

Hong Kong has a most unusual status in that part of the world. It was a British colony for over a hundred years, returning to Chinese control in 1997. It now has the status of "special administrative region," retaining a degree of autonomy and self-governance – although constantly contending with the mainland. Hong Kong has a long tradition as home to the triad criminal organizations (Chu 2000). It also has a strong history of combating both the triads and corruption; for which it has one of the most sophisticated and well-resourced operations in the world (Lo 1993). According to the élite Organized Crime and Triad Bureau of the Hong Kong Police, some of the leading organized crime problems in Hong Kong are vehicle crime and smuggling, human smuggling, cross-border organized crime involving China and Macau, money laundering, drug trafficking, debt-collection, and triad monopolies, including the control by triad societies of private bus routes, fish markets, street markets, wholesale markets, entertainment centers, parking services, fake VCD sales, prostitution, illegal gambling, and extortion. The major criminal groups – the Wo Shing Wo, the San Yee On, and the 14K – are said to be involved in the manufacture and street-level distribution of pirated VCDs and DVDs. As a major transportation and financial center of Asia and a transit point for China, Hong Kong has been a hub for transnational organized crime activities for the past thirty years. Today, it continues to be an *entrepôt* for the illicit movement of goods, services, and people to and from the mainland.

Colombian drug cartels, guerillas, and paramilitaries

Colombia, a much-troubled Latin American country, has a long-standing reputation as a global center of cocaine production and trafficking, and a major supplier of heroin to the United States, Ecuador, Venezuela, Nicaragua, Guatemala, and Mexico. Europe, Australia, and certain African countries have also been important customers. Colombia has an unfortunate reputation: not only as a home to drug cartels, but also to corruption, guerillas, paramilitaries, and pervasive violence. Colombia has one of the highest rates of violence of any country in the world (see, for example the UN *Global Report on Crime and Justice*, 1999).

Earlier, I discussed the difference between *mala in se* and *mala prohibita* crimes. Another term that has been used for the latter is "non-conventional crimes," including many forms of organized crime (for example, human trafficking and money laundering), high-level corruption, terrorism, and cyber-crimes. The UN Center for International Crime Prevention has created an index of non-conventional crimes, scoring and ranking different countries on how much they have. In one such ranking, of seventy-four countries, Colombia had the undesirable distinction of being first – meaning it has a greater problem with non-conventional crime than any other country in the world. What accounts for this sorry situation? The answers are complicated and include certain cultural and historical traditions that are said to resemble those of Sicily and Southern Italy:

> With a socio-historical background paralleling that of Southern Italy, the cultural ethos underpinning the Colombian

"narco-mafia" – the traditions of violence, the strong family ties, the long history of social banditry and extortion, the distrust of government, and the combination of criminal and entrepreneurial skills – resembles those of the Sicilian Mafia and *La Cosa Nostra*. Also, as has been true of Sicily, Colombia provides a friendly refuge for launching or incubating organized crime.

Pennsylvania Crime Commission, (1991:255).

In the early 1970s, drug traffickers from Colombia supplied cocaine to other organized crime groups, such as LCN and various Mexican and Cuban gangs. Later, when the cocaine business became hugely profitable, some of the traffickers decided to take an even bigger market share, by running their own smuggling and distribution operations. They formed "drug cartels," or independent trafficking organizations. The two largest and best known

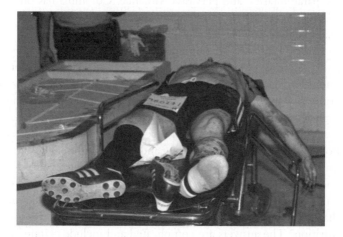

Figure 11 The body of Colombian drug lord Helmer Herrera lies in a hospital morgue, 200 miles southwest of Bogota, Colombia. The former third-ranking member of the Cali drug cartel, Herrera was shot and killed by a lone gunman while playing soccer in prison, where he had been sentenced for drug trafficking (AP Photo/SilvanaBuitrago).

were the Cali and Medellin cartels (named after the Colombian cities in which they were based). These cartels were extremely complex, corporation-like structures, which employed thousands of people (one estimate put the number at 24,000) and did billions of dollars-worth of business.

The Cali and Medellin cartels were effectively dismantled by law enforcement agencies in the 1990s. Since then, these criminal mega-organizations have been replaced by much smaller and lower profile criminal groups. One is the Juvenal Group: comprised of around 260 people, for the most part with professional or business backgrounds, and without criminal records, this group does not attempt to control all aspects of the drug trafficking business, as the earlier cartels did. They subcontract out to Mexican, Venezuelan, Ecuadorian, and other groups, a situation not unlike that before the rise of the cartels. As an example of the transnational coordination between other criminal organizations and the Juvenal and other drug groups, an alleged member of the Italian mafia was recently arrested in Colombia for arranging cocaine shipments to Europe (UN *Global Studies on Organized Crime*, 2000).

The original Colombian cartels exhibited many of the characteristics of organized crime groups. They controlled the prices of drugs, they eliminated competition, they avoided prosecution through the use of violence and corruption, and they used other criminal activities and legitimate businesses to hide and launder their huge drug profits. Drug money was used to bribe law enforcement officials, judges, politicians, and lawyers. As is the case with other organized crime groups, for a long time bribery crippled law enforcement efforts against the cartels. The traffickers were willing to kill anyone who turned against them, or moved against them, including a presidential candidate, an attorney general, legislators, judges, prosecutors, police officials, journalists, and others. Ultimately, the audacity of some of the cartel leaders, their promiscuous use of violence, and external political pressures on the Colombian government combined to bring them down. The newer drug groups, such as Juvenal, are said to avoid violence, so as to avoid police detection, but they rely heavily on corruption to facilitate their criminal activities. Although smaller organizations, they still have large profits – an estimated $300 million a year for Juvenal – that they invest within the legal economy.

Drug trafficking, and a wide variety of other crimes, are also associated with the major leftist guerilla groups, such as the Revolutionary Armed Forces of Colombia, the largest of the rebel groups fighting the Colombian government. (The next largest is the National Liberation Army.) Although these rebels ostensibly have an ideological purpose – the overthrow of the existing government – they use drug trafficking as a source of income. Similarly, the paramilitary groups, formed in the 1980s by drug smugglers and cattle ranchers to protect them from leftist guerillas, have been linked to the cocaine trade, and to some of the worst atrocities of the forty-year guerilla war, including massacres and kidnapping, as well as drug smuggling.

All this has resulted in a highly dangerous, volatile, and lawless environment, riddled with crime and corruption. Innocent villagers are massacred, business and professional people and their families are kidnapped for ransom, and police officers are regularly murdered. (Colombia is one of the most unsafe places in the world to be a police officer.) Organized criminality, as I saw for myself in a visit to Colombia several years ago, seems to have reached its apex here. Anyone who is naïve enough to believe that organized crime does not harm anyone if they have no dealings with it should visit Colombia.

As this series of global snapshots clearly shows, organized crime has many faces, of which the traditional mafia is only one. Criminal organizations arise out of various economic, social and political conditions. What they do, and how they do it, will be the subject of the next two chapters.

5

Organized crime is what organized crime does

We have considered at length what organized crime is, looked at who the criminals (gangsters, mobsters, or racketeers) are, and at why they might have become what they are. We have also looked briefly at what these particular criminals do and how they do it. It is to these, the businesses of organized crime, which we now return.

One of the most basic assertions that can be made about organized crime is that it exists to make money. At its core, it is an economic enterprise (usually many economic enterprises) driven by greed and the desire to "make a quick buck" without, as the saying goes, "doing too much heavy lifting." Organized crime has no politics or ideology; thus differing from terrorist organizations, even though they may share methods and tactics. When organized crime enters the political realm, such as putting up candidates for public office (in Russia and Taiwan), it does so solely to further its economic interests. The fundamental reality that enables organized crime to achieve its goal of making money is, in a nutshell, human weaknesses, needs, and desires. Organized crime grows and sustains itself by supplying goods and services that are in demand, but are either illegal or in short supply.

In the case of dealing in stolen goods, the criminals are responding to their customers' desire to get something for nothing, or at least more cheaply than in the legitimate market. Selling stolen goods does not necessarily require a criminal organization but if such selling is to become a professional operation – a business – it requires the systematic theft of goods that are in demand and reliable outlets for disposing of them. For example, luxury cars are stolen on demand, moved to different locations, stored, repainted, and then delivered to the customers who ordered a Lexus, a Mercedes, or a BMW. The customer gets the car for below market price, but the organization effectively gets it for nothing, so the profit margin is quite good! It is reasonable to ask who is really at fault; who or what is the cause of this particular crime.

Illicit goods include babies, drugs, exotic animals and plants, illegal firearms, and stolen property. Illicit services include gambling, money laundering, and sex. First, we'll consider the diversity of illicit activities and markets that revolve around generally legal, but regulated or controlled, goods and products.

Profiting from the illegality of the otherwise legal

Short supply – meaning not enough of an otherwise legal product or service being available to meet the consumer demand – can result from regulation, for example, of alcohol and prescription drugs, or from inadequate or irregular supply. The sorts of businesses set up to meet this demand require organizational capability, capital to buy the product (unless they are dealing in stolen goods), ways to transport and store it, and a distribution system. This type of activity can be a very lucrative venture for criminal organizations. The key to making a profit is having customers anxious to buy regulated or taxed products for less than the normal retail price, without adhering to regulatory requirements.

Cigarettes are a good example of both regulation and irregular supply. In both Russia and the US, criminal groups have found ways of making money by getting around the government's cigarette tax policy. Much of the cost of a pack of cigarettes in the United States is made up of tax, which differs from one state and locality to another: handsome profits can be made by buying cigarettes in bulk from low-tax states and selling them below the market price in high-tax ones. In 1990s Russia, the Ziberman Group was heavily involved in both cigarette and alcohol smuggling (UN *CICP*: 117–18). This criminal group exploited special economic zones, created by the Russian government to provide tax incentives for the development of legitimate businesses.

Motor fuel (gasoline and diesel fuel) is also heavily taxed in the US Soviet émigré criminals made millions from selling bootleg (untaxed) gasoline in New York and New Jersey in the 1980s, from customers willing to buy gasoline from "no name" filling stations at prices far below the market price, with no questions asked. This scam was enormously profitable: four indictments made by the US Department of Justice, charging defendants from the former Soviet Union with the evasion of motor fuel excise taxes were for $14 million, $35 million, $60 million and $140 million (Finckenauer & Waring, 1998:246–247).

In many countries, imported luxury goods, such as designer clothing, perfumes, fine wines and spirits, and luxury cars, are subject to high tariffs or are not easily obtainable. If there is sufficient demand, a black market arises to supply these goods. The supplying requires organization, the willingness to take risks, and a customer base. Much of this sort of black market activity, although not necessarily all, becomes an enterprise of organized crime. Racketeers employ a cost/benefit equation: does the potential profit outweigh the costs (both in investment that must be made, and in the risks involved)?

Globally, a number of crimes associated with attempts to control certain products have burgeoned since the 1990s. These crimes are transnational, and given the sophistication and organizational capability required to carry them out successfully, are largely associated with transnational organized crime groups:

- *Trafficking in human organs*: increased demand for organ transplants, such as kidneys, limited supply, a growing reliance on living donors, and pressure for commercialization, has created a profitable market in human organs. Suffering patients, who may be close to death, but have the necessary funds, are willing to pay. Not surprisingly, this market is exploited by criminal organizations. Medical professionals are involved in "harvesting" the organs; in some cases victim "donors," including children, have been kidnapped in order to reap this grim harvest.

- *Trafficking in firearms*: small arms and light weapons are not illegal but their sale and distribution is highly regulated, especially the sale of arms to certain countries and areas that are experiencing civil conflicts and guerilla wars. The former Yugoslavia, West Africa, East Timor, and areas of Central, South, and South-West Asia are examples of areas where there has been a great demand for arms. Money can be made through the illicit transfer of arms from manufacturing countries such as the United States, Russia and China. These are transnational crimes requiring sophisticated and well-managed transport and storage systems, international contacts, and fraudulent documents; all within the purview and capability of organized crime. Of special concern with respect to weapons trafficking is the possibility of criminal organizations becoming involved in the trafficking of nuclear and other radioactive materials, or biological and chemical weapons. Terrorist organizations, rich in cash, might well use some of it to entice organized crime groups to procure such weapons of mass destruction.

- *Dealing in endangered species*: there is a growing international trade in protected species of exotic animals and plants. The demand (from zoos, private collectors, dealers, and others) exceeds the regulated supply. For example, the delicacy caviar comes from an endangered fish, the sturgeon. As a result of severe over-fishing and pollution, sturgeon stocks have become extremely depleted. Consequently, caviar has become tightly regulated – in fact, its production from the Caspian Sea has been outlawed. Nevertheless, the global demand for the best caviar, which comes only from the Caspian sturgeon, continues apace. The caviar-consuming market ignores long-term consequences in favor of short-term self-interest. There is money to be made from its illegal trade, and there are criminal organizations willing and able to make it.

• *Illegal logging*: to protect rainforests in the Amazon Basin in South America, Africa and Southeast Asia, and the extensive timberlands of Siberia from total destruction and elimination, logging and the removal of live trees is regulated and controlled. The legal supply is thus limited, but demand remains and, if anything, has increased. It has been estimated that the illegal logging is a \$10–\$15 billion per year industry (*A Revised Forest Strategy*, World Bank Group, October 2002). Exploiting the timber market requires the illegal cutting or removal of protected species of tree, corruption of the supposed regulators, money laundering, wood-processing, transport and shipment, customs paperwork, and so on. This is not a criminal activity for amateurs; it needs professional transnational criminal organizations.

• *Trafficking in hazardous waste*: the dangerous by-products of industrial activity must be disposed of carefully; a process that requires considerable regulation and licensing. It is cheaper, faster and easier for companies, or even governments, to get rid of hazardous wastes outside those regulations. Organized crime groups, with trucks and drivers, and without scruples, can and do profit from illegally disposing of hazardous materials. Among its other ills, this activity creates enormous environmental hazards and threats to human health as air, ground water and waterways are polluted.

• *Trafficking in cultural artifacts*: cultural artifacts, such as pottery, wood carvings, paintings, sculptures, religious icons and so on, have been brought more and more under protective national and international legislation in recent years, outlawing the removal and receipt of countries' national heritage. Such laws seek both to prevent the loss and destruction of the artifacts, and the exploitation by the rich countries of the West of the poor countries of Africa, Asia, Latin America, and the Middle East. According to a recent UN report, transnational trafficking networks have linked with local people in areas where there are valuable antiquities, and with dealers who want to buy and sell these antiquities (Secretary-General's Report, 2004). The local people steal items and sell them to the smugglers, who transport and sell them at a profit to dealers, who then sell them for even more profit to private collectors. Everybody benefits, except the countries whose national heritage is being looted.

As lucrative as this particular business is, it is only one of the many kinds of trafficking in cultural properties in which organized crime groups may be involved. Another peculiarly twenty-first century activity is the pirating of artistic and literary works. The Wo Shing Wo Triad in Hong Kong is reported to be extensively involved in the manufacturing and street selling of pirated VCDs and DVDs (Chu, 2005). The pirating of copyrighted material, such as movies, songs, television shows, and even books, is a huge activity in mainland China, but just how much of it involves true organized groups is not known.

• *Financial crimes, cyber-crime and Internet scams*: organized crime has penetrated the global financial system. Banking and insurance frauds, identity theft, credit card frauds, international money laundering, computer fraud, computer-related forgery, and copyright infringement are just some of the financial crimes engaged in by sophisticated criminal groups: all crimes made possible by advances in computer technology.

Another crime in this category is child pornography. The trafficking of children to feed the demand is a horrible enough crime, but there are many other horrible aspects to the business itself. As long as there is a demand from pedophiles, having a controlling interest in child pornography websites, the making and distributing of pornographic films, running sex tours, and so on, is big business.

The increasing use of the Internet for direct retail businesses, where customers buy over the web using credit cards, or use Internet-based payment systems for hotel reservations, car rental and so on, makes these businesses highly vulnerable to victimization by organized crime. This is especially true for online gambling sites: Internet gambling not only can be a revenue source for organized crime, but also creates opportunities for loan sharking.

All these crimes are international, although there is nothing to prevent them being carried out strictly within national borders. In many respects, they represent the new face of organized crime – global, high-tech and sophisticated. But that does not mean that gangsters have given up the old mainstays. Forerunners to, yet contemporary with these "new" criminal activities, is a litany of crimes that involve the provision of unquestionably illegal goods and services. For many years, until the 1990s, these crimes provided the bread and butter for organized crime. And they still do, for many criminal organizations in many areas.

At the core of organized crime are the principles of supply and demand. However, in certain instances, organized crime creates (or "pumps up") a particular demand. If we consider some examples of the goods and services which organized crime purveys, we will see how the demand and supply equation works.

Organized crime exploits sin

Human desires, morals, laws, and crime intersect, and sometimes clash, in a host of gray areas. Within their different legal and moral codes, most countries struggle either to eliminate a particular behavior (such as prostitution), to control or regulate it in some way (for example, casino gambling), and/or to profit from it (for example, government-run lotteries). Their efforts are at best only ever partially successful; it is in the criss-crossing of desire/demand and control/supply that organized crime seizes the opportunity to make money.

Gambling, sex, and drugs are the clearest examples of how organized crime fulfills human desire for forbidden fruit. Tied to gambling is another money maker for organized crime: loan sharking. A third example is the fencing of stolen goods.

Gambling is ubiquitous, and probably as old as humankind. It is conducted in a great variety of ways, limited only by human imagination. Much gambling activity has no connection to organized crime – for example, bingo games. Gambling is a topic that divides people into two opposing camps. On one side are those who see gambling as harmless fun and entertainment that doesn't hurt anyone: if mature adults want to take chances with their own money, they should be allowed to and governments should not try to legislate for personal morality. On practical economic grounds, it is further argued that gambling brings jobs and economic revival to otherwise poor or depressed areas, for example, on Native American reservations in the United States. On the other side are those who view gambling as sinful, responsible for destroying homes and lives, or as the province of mobsters.

Policy makers who have tried to carve a path between these two views have generally focused on the latter two issues. Public educational messages, and treatment for gambling addiction, balance political support for controlled gambling. In addition, it is argued that stringent law enforcement will prevent, or combat, infiltration by organized crime. To assess the possibilities of this claim, we will consider some ways in which organized crime is involved in gambling:

- *Bookmaking*: betting on the outcome of sporting events such as horse races, boxing matches, basketball, football and baseball games, or World Cup soccer is an extremely popular form of gambling. Betting is usually done according to "the line": the probability (or odds) of a predicted outcome. For example, in a championship boxing match, the odds will favor either the champion or the challenger. If the champion is favored by 3:1, that means that if he wins, people who bet on that outcome win one dollar for every three dollars they laid out. If on the other hand, the challenger wins, those who bet on him get three dollars for every one dollar bet.

  Bookmakers accept bets from individuals. Bets may be placed by telephone, via a middleman such as a bartender, a waitress or a barber, or increasingly, via the Internet. Gambling profits accrue from the difference between the amounts lost by the losers and the amounts won by the winners. Bookmakers make their money by taking a cut from this difference.

  Organized crime enters into bookmaking by providing a "lay off" service. If bookmakers get many bets on one outcome for a particular event, such that if that outcome occurs they will be unable to pay all the winnings, they may lay off some of these bets (that is, themselves make bets with another bookmaker, to reduce their liabilities).

- *Numbers racket*: a form of lottery, in which people place bets on a group of numbers. Bets are usually placed in small local businesses, such as bars or grocery stores, although the Internet is now a major tool for this form of lottery. Bets are taken every day and there is a pay-off every day. Organized crime makes its money from the numbers/lottery either by providing a lay-off service (necessary when one particular number receives so many bets that if it were to win the local operator would be unable to pay), or through imposing a "mob" or "street" tax (a fee paid for the privilege of being allowed to operate the numbers racket in mob territory).

- *Video poker games*: now often found in bars, taverns, snack bars, and truck stops. Organized crime groups install the machines whether the owner wants them or not, but usually split the profits, which can amount to several thousand dollars per machine per week.

- *Casinos and casino gambling*: the high-class end of the gambling world. Many resort (or aspiring resort) areas in cities around the world either already have or are developing casinos. In addition to first-rate entertainment, five star hotel rooms and excellent restaurants, these casinos offer all varieties of gambling – slot machines, blackjack tables, poker tables, roulette wheels and so on. Despite strong claims from US casino cities, such as Las Vegas and Atlantic City, that they have no organized crime presence, there is evidence of such involvement (see for example, Anastasia, 1991). That involvement can come either as silent or hidden partner ownership, or directly from the skimming of money from the gambling profits. It can also come from controlling the unions that represent the casino workers: croupiers, bartenders, waiting staff, janitorial staff, and so on. Prostitution, drug dealing, and unauthorized gambling are often found in the areas surrounding casinos; casinos are good for all these businesses, which are often controlled by organized crime.

In its study of transnational criminal organizations (*Trends in Organized Crime*, Winter 2000) the United Nations found that a number of these organizations, especially Chinese organized crime groups, had gambling as one of their criminal activities. One example described in the UN report was the Savlokhov

Group, in Ukraine. Among its list of businesses, the Savlokhov leadership owned a number of gambling establishments. These, as well as their restaurants, car dealerships and filling stations, produced legal income, but were also used to further their illicit activities, such as money laundering, loan sharking, and usury. Loan sharking, usury and gambling frequently go hand-in-hand.

- *Loan sharking*: lending money at usurious rates of interest, or rates above the legally-permitted level, is a major business for many criminal organizations. In Dwight Smith's "spectrum of enterprise" theory of organized crime, loan sharking is a perfect illustration of how this particular criminal enterprise works. The demand to borrow money is usually met by banks, credit or lending companies, or friends and family. The government establishes the maximum interest rate that can be charged for the use of this borrowed money, and makes it a crime (usury) to exceed that rate. The formal lending agencies usually require some form of security (for example, property) against which to guarantee the loan's repayment. This system normally works well and satisfies most borrowers' needs

  However, some potential borrowers are a very poor credit risk. They may have no job, or only a low-paying job; they perhaps own no property and thus can offer no security; or they may have previously defaulted on loans. This means lenders – perhaps including their families – are highly unlikely to make them a loan. The potential borrower has two choices: they can give up on whatever the loan was to be used for, or they can turn to a source outside the legitimate stream. This is where loan sharking and organized crime can come in.

  To further complicate matters, but to capture what realistically is quite often the case, imagine the borrower needs the loan to pay gambling losses and debts, or to buy drugs. Legitimate lending institutions are highly unlikely to be forthcoming;

thus, the borrower must get their loan from an illicit source, which will cost them dearly.

Loan sharks operate within the ambit of organized crime because they need a ready supply of funds, and because they need the reputation for violence that will insure repayment. Their particular borrowers are not the most reliable of clients, and any loan shark who is unable to enforce a repayment schedule will soon be out of business. Thugs make sure that does not happen.

- *The sex industry*: like gambling, this extends far back into human history. Different countries have different laws regulating, and in some cases prohibiting, commercial prostitution establishments. In the United States, brothels or houses of prostitution are outlawed, except in certain places in Nevada, although, of course, that does not mean that brothels do not exist anywhere else. In other countries, such as Taiwan and the Netherlands, prostitution is legal but controlled. Many cities in different countries have "red light districts" for prostitution, for example, Amsterdam, Bangkok, Manila, and Tokyo.

Brothels, massage parlors, and topless bars are all highly likely to be either wholly or partially owned or controlled by criminal organizations, or pay protection money to them. Because drug use frequently accompanies activities in such establishments, drug dealing can often be a lucrative ancillary enterprise. Pimps, the "business" managers of streetwalkers, call girls, and prostitutes, are either controlled by criminal gangs, or must hand over a percentage of their profits from the business.

In the pornography business, and especially child pornography, organized crime both collects money from the operations themselves and extorts money from users, who are blackmailed and threatened with exposure if they do not pay.

While researching the problem of the trafficking of Chinese women for the sex industry in Taiwan, a colleague and I observed a police raid on a sex club in Taipei. The club itself was not illegal: the raid was to determine if there were any Chinese women who had illegally migrated to Taiwan working there. There were not – or at least not any who were still there by the time we and the police arrived. This incident exemplifies a significant connection between organized crime and the sex industry: the trafficking of women, and in some cases children, to supply the industry. I shall return to this issue in the next chapter.

Drug trafficking – the king of the hill

Last, but by no means least of the illicit businesses, is what is now considered to be by far the biggest money maker for organized crime today: drugs. Use of mood-altering or narcotic substances is a long-standing human activity. The indigenous peoples of areas where such substances originate have long made use of them for a variety of purposes: medicinal, religious, recreational, and so on. The natural substances they use include the poppy plants from which opium and heroin are derived, the coca shrubs from which comes cocaine, and the hemp plant that is the source of cannabis, or marijuana.

It is an interesting geopolitical phenomenon that the locations from which most of these substances are derived are not those in which most of the consumption takes place. Thus, as well as the basic consumer demand, an important factor linking drugs to organized crime is the organizational capacity needed to get the product from its source to its consumers. First, the crop must be farmed; someone must plant it, nurture it, and harvest it. This requires capital and people (and if local law enforcement is pressing, bribery). Second, once the crop has been harvested, it must be moved, stored, and processed or refined into its consumable form. Third, the refined product – heroin, cocaine, or marijuana – must be shipped via wholesalers to the retailers. This requires transport, distribution, and accounting systems. Finally, once the product is in the hands of the retailers – the street dealers – there must be a system to insure that profits are passed back up the chain and that all necessary payments are made and accounted for.

This vastly simplified overview nonetheless makes the point that drug trafficking is not a crime that can be successfully carried out by "unorganized" criminals. Not only does it require a criminal organization, but because the sources of supply and the most lucrative markets are in different regions, it requires transnational criminal organization.

The major sources of heroin are in two "golden" areas: the Golden Triangle, which runs through Laos, Myanmar (Burma) and Thailand in Southeast Asia, and the Golden Crescent, which encompasses parts of Pakistan, Afghanistan, and Iran in Central Asia. The Golden Triangle is a large, but politically isolated, area. Largely jungle, the rule of law is weak, law enforcement is lax, and corruption is rampant. Myanmar alone is said to account for ninety per cent of heroin production in the Golden Triangle. Part of the country is governed by the Wa Army, for which heroin is a major source of income (see box).

Afghanistan, in the Golden Crescent, is considered to be the world's largest producer of heroin. Although heroin production dropped off sharply during the Taliban regime, in the aftermath of the Coalition invasion of Afghanistan in 2001 it has risen to very high levels. The countries of the Golden Crescent, like those of the Golden Triangle, have troubled economic circumstances and volatile political situations. Heroin is an extremely profitable product: the money that flows from consumers to the producers and their protectors sustains many families, but it also sustains warlord armies, guerilla operations and, some would argue, terrorist organizations.

Two other countries heavily linked to transnational heroin trafficking are Colombia and Mexico. Both (with Jamaica) are also major sources of marijuana; Colombia, in addition, is the world's pre-eminent supplier of cocaine. Like poppies and heroin, to operate a successful cocaine business criminal entrepreneurs must have the sophisticated organizational capacity to farm, harvest and refine coca into cocaine, then store and distribute it to major cities around the world. Once again, transnational criminal organizations are required: the principal markets for heroin and cocaine are, not surprisingly, the world's rich countries; the United States, the countries of western Europe, Australia and Japan. The demand for these drugs, and the ability to pay handsomely for them, fuels the transnational drug business.

In the US, before 1960, the demand for drugs was relatively sporadic and small. Heroin use was more or less confined to ghettos in cities like New York. Although organized crime groups, such as the Sicilian Mafia, were the wholesalers, the street supply could be sustained by low-level criminals acting as individual entrepreneurs. After 1960, the social climate, and the knowledge about and the attitudes toward drugs began to change dramatically. The demand for drugs (and thus the opportunities for drug dealing) and the profits to be made, increased substantially. The United States began to become the world's principal market for drugs and the target of international drug cartels.

A new class of drugs began to appear in the 1960s: synthetic or "designer" drugs, including "uppers" like methamphetamines (meth, crystal meth, ice, speed), PCP, Ecstasy, and LSD, and barbiturates or "downers." Outlaw motorcycle gangs, such as the Hells Angels, are major players in the synthetic drug market, especially for methamphetamines. See the box for an illustration of the growth and character of the methamphetamine business in an excerpt from a report by Ko-lin Chin on his research in the Golden Triangle.

THE OPIUM TRADE IN THE WA AREA OF THE GOLDEN TRIANGLE

This study examined the social organization and social processes of opium cultivation, heroin production, drug use, and drug distribution within an area of the Golden Triangle.

The study found that the emergence of the "speed" (methamphetamine) business has completely transformed the drug market in the Golden Triangle. Before, only a relatively small number of people were involved in the opium and heroin trade and most of them relied on it to survive, rather than to get rich. The Thai authorities were not concerned, because the impact was restricted to poor people in the north or drug addicts abroad. However, with the introduction of speed in the mid-1990s, many people who otherwise would not have participated in the drug trade have now been recruited. This has changed the Thai authorities' attitudes, because in Thailand speed is mainly consumed by young people. The Thai authorities have begun to be aggressive in combating the problem; speed dealers now regularly receive death sentences. The Thai government became so concerned with the methamphetamine epidemic that it launched a massive crackdown on speed dealers in 2003; within a few months, more than two thousand *yaba* dealers were shot and killed in the streets by unknown gunmen.

Considering the magnitude of the drug problem and how deeply it is embedded in this area, the conclusion is that the prevention programs and suppression programs being initiated are unlikely to have any significant impact. Unless the world community makes a concerted effort and implements a well-integrated, well-financed economic program to improve drastically the lives of these poor ethnic peoples, there is little hope of creating drug-free zones in these areas. For ordinary people, soldiers, and government officials in Wa State, growing opium, and producing heroin and methamphetamine are the only options available to make money. When there are no other alternatives for them to sustain themselves, it is only natural for them to keep on doing what they are used to and good at.

Ko-lin Chin, Principal Investigator, National Science Foundation Project, 2004.

A global survey of forty organized crime groups in sixteen countries made by the United Nations (*Trends in Organized Crime*, Winter 2000), found that a significant proportion had drug trafficking as their main or core criminal activity. Examples include two German groups: one situated in the Bremen and Bremerhaven region, which trafficked cocaine and marijuana from Venezuela to Germany, and one in the Saxony region, which trafficked heroin from Turkey to Germany. The Netherlands also reported two major drug trafficking organizations moving hashish into the Randstadt (comprising The Hague, Rotterdam, Amsterdam and Utrecht). Australia and Canada reported outlaw motorcycle gangs producing and distributing amphetamines and cannabis.

Perhaps the biggest among the reported groups were three organized crime groups from Mexico. (All three have since been either dismantled or their activities sharply curtailed.) The Amezcua Contreras Organization was one of the leading smugglers of ephedrine (a key ingredient in the production of methamphetamine), and was reported to be the largest producer and trafficker of methamphetamine in the world. A truly international operation, the Amezcua had contacts for obtaining ephedrine in Switzerland, India, Germany, the Czech Republic, and Thailand. More than one hundred strong, they also dealt in the cocaine business, and not surprisingly, their principal sales outlet was the United States. The Carillo Fuentes Organization transported large cocaine shipments from Colombia to the United States, and also trafficked in heroin and marijuana. At their peak, this group reportedly made tens of millions of dollars in profits per week. Finally, the Arellano-Felix Organization was one of the most violent drug cartels known to the authorities at that time. For more than a decade, they controlled the flow of drugs (cocaine, heroin, cannabis, and methamphetamine) across the border between San Diego, California and Tijuana, Mexico. As well as using violence, Arellano-Felix sustained a network of corrupted law enforcement officials and was involved in kidnappings. They were thought to use a sophisticated system of counter-surveillance to protect their operations.

Like the gambling and sex businesses, drug trafficking is sustained and profitable because there is a demand. The United States government has been criticized for over-emphasizing and focusing too closely on the supply side of drugs and for not doing enough, in either policy or practice, to try to reduce the demand. Whatever the merits of the arguments in this debate, and their applicability in different countries, it is clear that international drug trafficking continues to be a major business of transnational organized crime groups.

As if this panoply of illicit businesses were not enough, there is a third method by which organized crime operates as an economic enterprise. And in many ways, this is the most threatening and troubling.

Predatory crime

Part of their criminal repertoire of some of the more sophisticated of the criminal organizations, for example, *La Cosa Nostra*, *Yakuza*, and the Italian Mafia, is the infiltration of legitimate businesses. This is a particularly predatory or parasitic form of organized crime; because the criminals feed on and suck the life blood from legal economic enterprises. However, this crime is not characteristic of all organized crime groups.

An example of this sort of crime is stock fraud. In one form, gangsters press legitimate stockbrokers to "push" shares of particular stocks in order to inflate their value artificially. These stocks are in businesses that are either wholly or partly owned by organized crime. Once the value of the stocks has been "pumped up," they are "dumped" (sold off) before prices plummet, giving the scheme its name: "pump and dump." The unwitting stockholders, who are left holding valueless stocks, are the ones who lose money. Stockbrokers go along with such illegal schemes simply because gangsters physically threaten them and their families if they refuse to cooperate. The threat of violence separates this from typical white-collar type crime.

More formal and general names for predatory activities are business and labor racketeering. The racketeers are not responding to a demand for something illicit or unavailable, but aggressively seek and attack weaknesses in the economic structure. For example, *La Cosa Nostra* has a long history of exploiting labor unions in the United States. In China and Russia, and in Japan's experience with *Yakuza*, are numerous examples of criminal organizations penetrating various businesses, assuming at least partial control and/or skimming the profits. The *Yamaguchi-Gumi* group in Japan is said to be heavily involved in the entertainment, real estate and construction businesses, in a variety of ways, from protection schemes, to being silent partners, to running front companies.

One of the ways in which criminal penetration takes place has become a fairly common occurrence in Russia. The protection scheme known as the *krysha* (roof system) is extensive. This system is often operated by criminal organizations that have the strength, and propensity and reputation for violence, to be credible as protectors. Imagine a small Russian business, such as a bakery, has a dispute with a contracted supplier; perhaps deliveries of flour and sugar are not arriving. Under "normal" business circumstances in most other countries, this kind of dispute would ultimately be resolved through the legal system, perhaps a suit alleging breach of contract. However, in Russia, it is highly probable that the supplier has an arrangement with a *krysha* for protection of his trucks, drivers, and warehouses. This means the bakery owner is faced with the daunting and intimidating task of dealing with the supplier's *krysha* in attempting to resolve the dispute. The obvious solution is for the baker to hire his own *krysha*; but although this may solve the immediate problem, it can create other, even bigger, problems. For example, in return for being retained by the bakery owner for protection, the *krysha* may demand a share of the business: suddenly the owner has a criminal gang as a partner. Such unwilling and unwanted partnerships can arise even more straightforwardly, when a criminal organization threatens a restaurant or other business owner with violence and destruction if they do not turn over a certain share of their business to the organization. This is an obvious form of extortion.

Organized crime groups traditionally have varied motives for wanting to penetrate the legitimate economy. Profitable businesses such as pizza restaurants, dry cleaning establishments, catering businesses, and so on, can be a clean source of income. Businesses that are heavily regulated and require licensing, such as liquor stores or pharmacies, are avoided. Cash businesses, where there is quick turnover, and that have minimal accounting, can also be used for laundering the profits from illegal businesses. They provide a tax cover in which illegal income, perhaps from drug sales, is reported as profit from the legal business. Legal businesses can also provide "employment" for mobsters, usually as virtual jobs: in other words, they are on the books mostly for tax purposes. Any fan of the television show *The Sopranos* has seen a group of mobsters, day after day, relaxing, eating, drinking, and playing cards at a construction site – this is not a fantasy. Infiltration and ownership of a legal business also serves a third, important, purpose; providing a veneer of respectability. An organized crime boss seeking to be accepted in polite society – and to have his wife and children accepted – has to have an honorable profession. A legal business provides this facade. In the real world, the Gambino family boss, John Gotti, claimed to be a plumbing supply salesman; in the fictional world, Tony Soprano is supposedly employed in waste management.

Describing the sordid history of labor racketeering by *La Cosa Nostra* in the US, Jacobs (2006) explains how, over many years, gangsters penetrated labor unions to exploit them in a variety of ways. A combination of large union pension funds, the vulnerability of certain industries to the possibility of strikes by workers, and the special nature of certain goods and products (for example, fresh fish that are at high risk of rapid decay) made certain unions and the industries in which union members worked an attractive target for mob control.

Jacobs describes the various ways in which LCN gained access to the labor union's money. They force their way into jobs as union officials, where they draw excessive or multiple salaries; put family, friends, and mistresses on the payroll; gain access to union-owned expense accounts, cars, planes, and boats; and embezzle union funds. They extort money, called strike insurance, from employers by threatening strikes and walkouts and they force employers to buy goods and services from mob-owned or mob-controlled suppliers. A construction business, for example, has trucks that need gas – the owners can be forced to buy that gas only from mob-owned gas stations. That business needs enormous supplies of wood products – this supply can be obtained only from mob-controlled lumber yards, and so on. The key to organized crime's ability to do this is the omnipresent threat of violence. Resistant union officials or members are simply beaten up or killed. The strange disappearance of former Teamsters' International President, Jimmy Hoffa, is highly likely to have been an example of this use of violence. Employers are threatened with the destruction of their property and their products, and ultimately of their livelihood.

The harmful effects of this sort of labor racketeering are massive and insidious. Union members lose any voice in governing their own unions and thus have to take whatever they are given in contract negotiations. They lose their job security, as only mob favorites and sympathizers get rewarded. The pension funds they are counting on for retirement are stolen. And if they protest, they and their families can suffer violent consequences. For the public, mob monopolization of industries such as the trucking business, through their control of the International Brotherhood of Teamsters union, results in higher prices for every product that travels by truck. The same is true of the garment industry (clothing costs more), wholesale foods (food costs more), and the construction industry (building costs more). Taxpayers are forced to pay highly for shoddy and slipshod work on public works contracts, which produce low-quality and sometimes dangerous structures. Schools, public buildings, bridges, tunnels rapidly deteriorate, and structures fall down. This has historically been a huge problem in Sicily, and there is a fear that it will become so in China. If this were not bad enough, the siphoning off of pension funds provides a ready source of investment for criminal organizations to expand their illegal businesses.

This kind of predatory racketeering obviously cannot be accomplished by just any criminal organization. Effectively infiltrating the labor and business sectors requires considerable capacity to harm, which means criminal sophistication, a stable structure with a division of labor, and a credible reputation for reliability and violence. As Jacobs has pointed out (see *Gotham Unbound*, 1999), these mobsters have to be more than thugs; they must have "general business acumen." Among other things, this can mean taking a slice of a business, but not the whole pie; otherwise they would be stuck with having actually to manage the business. To most effectively exploit these kinds of market vulnerabilities, Jacobs says a criminal organization must be "entrepreneurial," "opportunistic," and "adaptable." These would all be examples of their degree of sophistication.

For criminal organizations such as *La Cosa Nostra*, *Yakuza*, the Sicilian Mafia and a few others, their penetration into the legitimate economy provides a bridge between the underworld and the upperworld. They operate an array of illegal enterprises, and also own or invest in an array of legal businesses. The Japanese *Yakuza* in Australia profits from drug and arms trafficking, gambling, extortion, money laundering, and prostitution, but also

Figure 5 A business of organized crime – slot machines seized by police in a gambling raid.

engages in labor racketeering, and has investments in nightclubs, restaurants, entertainment complexes, and golf courses (*Trends in Organized Crime*, Winter 2000:107–08). Casinos are a particularly attractive and versatile investment for these organized crime groups. This bridge brings not only the appearance of legitimacy, but also practical links to the worlds of business and politics. "Businesspeople," unlike common criminals, belong to the best clubs and rub elbows with the power brokers of society. Politicians and corporate executives, who would shy away from being seen in public with mobsters, are less anxious about dealing with businesspeople. The only reason they associate with them at all is simply because money talks: the huge funds accumulated by the most successful gangsters can be a major source of investments, loans, campaign funding, and electoral support.

Although shrouded in the mists of history and awash with allegations and innuendo, the story of the Kennedy family and the mob is a possible case of politicians and mobsters working with one another (see for example, English, 2005:259–289). The conspiratorial thread links the father, Joseph Kennedy, with bootlegging and various associations with organized crime figures to the son, President John F. Kennedy, sharing a girlfriend with Chicago mob boss Sam Giancana, to the celebrity spotlight, with the mob-tainted singer Frank Sinatra and his cronies, to the recruitment of racketeer bosses to assassinate Cuban leader Fidel Castro. Conspiracy theorists have long believed this web of intrigue might have caught up with President Kennedy and led to his assassination in 1963. A further historical twist is that a small-time hoodlum, Jack Ruby, murdered Kennedy's accused assassin, Lee Harvey Oswald.

There are numerous documented cases of this sort of symbiotic relationship (although perhaps not quite so dramatic) between organized crime, and business and politics. In Taiwan, *heijin* (black gold) refers to the intricate web of overlapping relationships among business, politics, and organized crime (Chin, 2003). Most businesses or professions in Taiwan are affiliated with gangsters who mediate in disputes and assist in the rigging of bids that enables businesses to win government contracts. According to Chin, the "real" godfathers in Taiwan are not the criminals engaged in traditional organized crimes, such as extortion; the most powerful and influential criminals make their money from the services they provide to big business. The country's power brokers wear three hats – business executive, political leader, and godfather. Because buying votes is so common in Taiwanese politics, the candidate who wishes actually to receive the votes for which he has paid must employ gangsters to visit voters and do the buying. This insures that he gets what he has paid for. Gangsters are also useful and necessary to protect against the campaign violence that is so prevalent in Taiwan.

Elsewhere, Guilio Andreotti, seven times prime minister of Italy, was prosecuted for a long-standing alliance with Italian mafia groups. Various criminal organizations in Russia have run and elected candidates to political office. As well as the Kennedy family connection in the United States, there have been a number of other instances in US history in which political machines and mobsters have worked together. In these cases, organized crime provides money, people, or other services in return for favorable laws, political appointments, immunity, lucrative public contracts, and that most ephemeral of benefits: respectability. The ultimate harm to society is, of course, incalculable.

Vulnerabilities and potential markets

I shall examine the means for combating organized crime in the concluding chapter; as a precursor, let us end this discussion by considering whether, with respect to the kinds of illicit businesses I have just detailed, there are certain vulnerabilities, economic conditions, or other factors that can help predict where and how organized crime might appear. Haller (1992) and Albanese (2004) have both looked at this issue. Haller argued that to discern the factors that cause, or at least facilitate, the involvement of organized crime in particular businesses, we should ask three questions:

- What are the economic conditions that shape particular illicit enterprises?

  Albanese proposed that at least one condition is the local standard of living. A low standard of living is a risk factor for participation in illegal activity, for example, gambling. Poverty and unemployment can be a stimulus to the growth of gambling in poor neighborhoods and certain kinds of gambling, such as the numbers racket, provide direct employment. And, of course, there is the ever-present dream of every gambler of winning the big jackpot. Although gambling is not necessarily related to organized crime, often it is.

Drug trafficking is also a source of jobs for the unskilled and the uneducated, and drugs provide a means of psychological escape. Loan sharking arises in response to the presence of poor financial risks, especially prevalent in poor neighborhoods.

The structure and nature of employment can also influence a community's vulnerability to organized crime. For instance, labor racketeering exists only or mainly where there are unions and unionized industries. However, non-professional or blue-collar unions are much more vulnerable to penetration than professional or white-collar unions.

- What are the geographical factors that bear on the location of particular criminal enterprises?

This implies there are unique or particular conditions in certain neighborhoods, cities, and even countries, which either facilitate or impede the development of criminal markets. I saw in Tel Aviv that the concentration of contract workers (young, unat-tached, males mostly from African countries) living in dormitory housing, led to the development of "massage parlors" nearby. These, in turn, were potential repositories for trafficking victims, and locations for prostitution and drug dealing. Countries with seaports and international airports are vulnerable to the businesses of transnational organized crime. An absence of economic development and economic opportunities creates fertile grounds for the growth of organized crime. Farmers will farm illegal crops, and young people will accept employment in illicit enterprises. With respect to geographical/environmental vulnerabilities, other risk factors include high demand for a particular product or service, affordable supply, and a competitive market for meeting that demand (Albanese, 2004). Further, Albanese argues that social changes, such as major political upheavals or changes in cross-border travel, and the introduction of new technology such as Internet access and cellphone availability, can create or expand criminal opportunities in particular locations.

- How do law enforcement policies affect the environments in which the businesses of organized crime are carried out? Would, for example, law enforcement crackdowns on certain criminal activities simply displace those activities to other areas, rather than eliminate them?

  Related structural risk factors include the level of training for law enforcement personnel for dealing with organized crime, police independence from politics, general police working conditions, and most important of all, the level of corruption. Both police corruption specifically, and political corruption more generally, are critical factors in deciding whether an environment is friendly or unfriendly to organized crime.

Organized crime is a business, or rather, a collection of businesses. Individual criminal organizations arise and thrive in response to market demands for illicit or limited goods and services, or their ability to penetrate the legitimate economic sector. Their success is determined by their reputation for and use of violence, their corruption of the legal and political systems, and their ability to control and dominate the particular criminal markets in which they are involved.

6

An evil business: the traffic in people

Three organized crime groups operating in ... Serbia are said to be trafficking women from Romania, Moldova, and Bulgaria and transporting them to Western European countries by land, air or sea. The three criminal groups buy prospective prostitutes in Eastern countries, transport them to the West, accustom them to the new surroundings, teach them what they have to do, and then sell them. The entire process is completed by recruiting prostitutes or, more rarely, luring innocent girls in Eastern European countries. This is done by local teams, which sell the girls ... for 500–1,500 Euros [a Euro is currently worth $1.20, meaning approximately 600–1800 dollars] each ... Girls, usually under the age of 23, cost 5,000–7,000 Euros each in Italy. The highest price paid for women in the West, specifically in Italy, is 10,000 Euros. Two of the [Serbian] groups also offer sexual services, since they have networks of pimps in a number of northern Italian towns, and the third group sells the women mostly to organized crime groups in Paris and Madrid

> BBC Monitoring International Reports,
> (November 22, 2003).

Because of the porosity of the US-Mexico border and the criminal networks that traverse it, the towns and cities along it have become the main staging area for an illicit and barbaric industry, whose "products" are women and girls. On both sides of the border, they are rented out for sex for as little as fifteen minutes at a time, dozens of times a day. Sometimes they are sold outright to

other traffickers and sex rings, victims and experts say. These sex
slaves earn no money, there is nothing voluntary about what they
do, and if they try to escape they are often beaten and sometimes
killed

> Peter Landesman, "The Girls Next Door,"
> (The New York Times, January 25, 2004).

These extracts, whose statistics have not been independently ver-
ified, capture some of the flavor and provide a revealing glimpse of
the seaminess of a booming criminal business: illegally transporting people (men, women, and children), largely across national
borders.

Trafficking is not a new business: it is as old as slavery and
human bondage. What is new are its increasing magnitude (both
in the number of people and the amount of money involved), the
number of countries affected, and the organization, sophistication
and sheer brutality of some of the traffickers. Because of the nature
and magnitude of the problems raised by human trafficking, perhaps the single most pressing issue is human rights and the gross
violations of those rights.

I have chosen to highlight and more closely examine this particular criminal business for a number of reasons: it has special supply and demand characteristics that illustrate how criminal
organizations exploit demands for illegal services; it has unique
victims – "reusable commodities" – that make it different from
drugs, timber, or other consumable commodities; it poses strong
moral questions about sex and values; it involves one of the oldest
professions – prostitution – but how that profession is being
exploited is very new; it is a transnational crime, with its own
stimuli; and finally, it illustrates very well the degree of involvement of traditional organized crime groups versus the involvement of more unstructured and/or informal criminal networks.
The last point is a matter of considerable controversy among
experts on human trafficking and organized crime, who disagree

over whether pointing to organized crime involvement is a way of highlighting the seriousness of the human trafficking problem to get more public attention.

The terminology

"Human smuggling" and "human trafficking" are often confused or used interchangeably, but they are not the same. Human smuggling arises from the desire of people to migrate from where they are to somewhere else. Migrating in search of a better life is not in itself a crime, as the United Nations *Protocol Against the Smuggling of Migrants* recognizes (see *Trends in Organized Crime*, Summer 2000:27). However, it is a crime to enter, or try to enter, a country without a valid entry visa or passport, including using a fake visa or passport. When a would-be migrant is unable to migrate legally – perhaps because they cannot get a valid visa – this is a classic example of a need or desire that cannot be met legally, and which stimulates an illegal solution. This situation can be, and often is, exploited by human smugglers.

Smuggling of migrants is defined as "[t]he procurement, in order to obtain, directly or indirectly, a financial or other material benefit, of the illegal entry of a person into a country of which the person is not a national or a permanent resident" (UNODC, 2006:6). It involves recruiting, transporting, harboring, or receiving people being moved illegally across national borders. The smugglers' profit from any of these transactions is usually short-term and single. People seeking to be smuggled must raise the necessary funds and pay the smugglers beforehand. Once they reach their destination, the smugglers have no further involvement. This mutual negotiation is not true of human trafficking, although trafficking cases often begin as smuggling cases. The "victims" want to migrate and agree to be smuggled: for example, a young woman who wants to go to another country to work as a nanny makes a contract with and pays a smuggler to help her. On arrival, the smuggler/trafficker tells her she owes an additional fee for food or other costs. Unable to pay, she is consigned to a brothel and forced into working as a prostitute. What began as smuggling becomes trafficking.

The US Trafficking Victims Protection Act of 2000 defines "severe forms of trafficking in persons" as:

> (a) sex trafficking in which a commercial sex act is induced by force, fraud, or coercion, or in which the person induced to perform such act has not attained 18 years of age; or (b) the recruitment, harboring, transportation, provision, or obtaining of a person for labor or services, through the use of force, fraud or coercion for the purpose of subjection to involuntary servitude, peonage, debt bondage, or slavery.

The United Nations *Protocol on Trafficking in Persons* (2000) similarly defines trafficking as:

> the recruitment, transportation, transfer, harboring or receipt of persons: *by the threat or use of kidnapping, force, fraud, deception or coercion* [italics added], or by giving or receiving or unlawful payments or benefits to achieve the consent of a person having control over another person, for the purpose of sexual exploitation or forced labor.

The use (or threat of use) of fraud, force, deception, or coercion against people held in forced labor, servitude, or slave-like conditions distinguishes smuggling and trafficking. Human trafficking profits from the unusual fact that people are expendable, re-usable, and re-sellable commodities.

Smuggling is relatively more voluntary; trafficking is involuntary. Trafficking "victims" do not choose to be victimized. These victims include women who agree to go to the United States, Japan, or Western Europe to work as waitresses, dancers, models, or *au pairs*, but are forced into prostitution or domestic servitude; children, who are abducted and sold abroad to work in pornography and prostitution rings, or as child labor; and migrant workers who are forced to work under slave-like conditions to pay their smuggling fees.

Despite their differences, human smuggling and human trafficking nevertheless may involve the same criminal actors. Putting aside the crucial distinction of the use of physical or psychological force and coercion, the organization and modes for recruiting, transporting, transferring, harboring, and receiving victims are almost the same. For all practical purposes, people who can do one can also do the other – and frequently they do.

Although trafficking can involve activities that take place within a country, I will focus on transnational criminal trafficking. This crime involves illegal acts, committed in more than one country, and which involve crossing national borders. Countries that are involved or implicated in trafficking (not all countries are) can be source, transit, or destination countries. Occasionally, a country is in more than one of these categories.

- *Source countries*, as the name implies, are the countries from which trafficking victims originate. They are usually, although not always, less-developed or developing countries, with weak economies and few job opportunities.
- *Transit countries* are those through which the trafficking victims pass. Transit countries usually have good transport links between source and destination countries, and/or are adjacent to the destination country. Transit countries often have other characteristics that facilitate or aid trafficking: for example, their national borders may be porous, because they are insecure or because of the corruption of those responsible for border security. They also have "safe houses" where victims can be held without the operations being bothered by law enforcement.

Mexico is a transit country for victims being trafficked into the United States from Central and South America, China and elsewhere. It is also a source country. The "coyotes," as the Mexican smugglers and traffickers are called, are not choosy about the nationality of their victims as long as they get paid. From Russia, it is reported that at any time there may be thousands (perhaps hundreds of thousands) of illegal Asians (mostly Chinese), Africans, Afghans, Kurds, and others in Moscow awaiting shipment to Western Europe and the United States. Like Mexico, Russia is also a source country for people being smuggled and trafficked.

- *Destination countries* are those to which the victims are taken. The most popular destinations are developed nations, such as the countries of Western Europe, Japan, Israel, Turkey, and the United States. These countries are relatively wealthy, have economic opportunities, and a demand for cheap labor. (In other words, the precise opposite of the source countries.) To the Chinese, the United States is *Jinshan*, or the Mountain of Gold (Chin, 1999); the land of opportunity. Ironically, some destination countries, such as Cambodia, Bosnia, and Pakistan do not seem to fit the profile of being economically desirable. We will examine this seeming anomaly shortly.

Source and destination countries have "push" and "pull" factors with respect to human trafficking. Push factors are the conditions in source countries that create an environment around, and a mental state in, potential victims that encourages and facilitates their victimization. People have strong reasons for wanting to leave their home countries. During a recent visit to China, I learned there were approximately 150 million "floating people" in just one area of China. These are mostly young people who have left their villages in search of opportunity. Depending on their degree of desperation, these young people – especially women – are a pool of potential trafficking victims. Other push factors include discrimination against women to the degree that they are treated as second class citizens and subject to abuse. Women seeking to escape the brutalities they experience under certain religiously fundamental regimes may be vulnerable to further victimization by traffickers. In countries such as Colombia, Myanmar, and Uzbekistan, civil strife and war force people from their homes and jobs, rendering them vulnerable to victimization. The same is true of natural disasters such as earthquakes and floods that destroy homes and livelihoods.

Pull factors are those that attract immigrants, therefore encouraging human smuggling. As well as economic opportunity, they can include the desire for political freedom, security, and safety. Ironically, pull factors may also create a lucrative market for human trafficking: for example, countries offering "sex tourism" – exploiting women, girls and boys to offer sexual pleasures to relatively wealthy businesspeople – need victims who can be coerced and forced into providing those pleasures. Countries with businesses and industries that seek "unprotected labor," that is, labor performed with no limits on working hours, no guaranteed minimum wage, no health benefits, or any pension plans or social security, also recruit and exploit trafficking victims.

The problem of human trafficking

Considerable efforts have been made to determine the scope of the trafficking problem, in terms of the numbers of trafficking victims. The questions of how many people and how much money is involved are currently not answerable. Trafficking is not a criminal offense in many countries, and in others it has only recently been made so, therefore arrest rates, prosecution and conviction data, traditionally relied on to give the magnitude of a crime problem are not generally available. Discrepancies in estimates of the numbers of trafficked victims in countries that do collect some statistics further suggest that the numbers we do have may not mean the same thing in different countries. This obviously makes the reaching of meaningful conclusions about the size of the problem extremely difficult.

As if the absence of reliable data were not bad enough, there is evidence that some of the data have been politicized; exploited for political purposes. Victims' service providers, non-governmental organizations (NGO) and women's groups have been primarily concerned with the harm caused to victims by trafficking. But some of these organizations have decided, often rightly, that for the problem to receive serious government attention it has to be presented and viewed in an alarming way. As has been true with similar social issues in the past, the issue must be so highlighted as to make ignoring it no longer politically feasible. The goal (to mix metaphors) is to "hold politicians' feet to the fire," in the belief that "the squeaky wheel gets the grease." Sex trafficking, in particular, has received a large amount of media attention: sex, violence and organized crime (usually portrayed as some form of mafia) – the ingredients that grab viewers' and readers' attention – are all there. The emotions aroused make it difficult to decide what is reality and what is being emphasized to get attention, or worse, for grisly entertainment.

This sort of politicizing partly accounts for the transformation of the trafficking problem from one of violations of human rights (as most non-governmental organizations see it) into an organized crime and illegal migration problem. The public, and public officials, are much more likely to be concerned about organized crime and illegal migration – which directly affect them and their constituents – than with the human rights of people (especially foreigners), some of whom are likely to be illegal aliens, prostitutes, or criminals. The organized crime aspect particularly attracts public attention and spurs governments into action. There has been a focus on defining the numbers of trafficking victims (particularly women) and on the profits gained from the trafficking business. It follows that a large number of trafficked people would perhaps indicate increases in irregular and illegal migration and increases in victimization.

The hefty profits estimated to be gained from trafficking have been presented as an indication of the involvement of organized crime networks. If there is a lot of money to be made illegally, it follows that organized crime would be interested. The organized crime networks linked to human trafficking have been portrayed as international in scope, very powerful, and as constituting threats to global security and peace. Human trafficking is said to be second only to drug trafficking in its degree of harm, and is regarded as being one of the most profitable illegal businesses for transnational organized crime (see for example, the *Trafficking in Persons Reports* of the US Department of State, 2001, et seq.).

The UN *Global Program Against Trafficking in Human Beings* has compiled a Trafficking Database (see the United Nations Office of Drugs and Crime website) made up of data reported from over a hundred sources. This compilation does not have any estimates of the actual numbers of trafficking victims but provides, for example, profiles of victims and the purposes behind their trafficking. Of the reported victims, seventy-seven per cent are said to be women, forty-nine per cent girls, and thirty-three per cent children. Only twelve per cent are boys, and nine per cent men. (These figures add up to more than one hundred per cent because one source can indicate more than one victim profile.) The vast majority (eighty-seven per cent) of victims are reported to be trafficked for sexual exploitation, and another twenty-eight per cent for forced labor. These estimates should be viewed in light of the earlier caution about how data are reported, by whom, and for what purposes.

The *2005 Trafficking in Persons Report* from the US State Department estimates the number of people trafficked annually across international borders to be 600,000 to 800,000. These figures come from a variety of sources: reports of specific trafficking incidents and repatriated victims, press reports, governmental and non-governmental reports, academic reports, and so on. Again, we must exercise caution in their interpretation. There is evidence that some smuggled people and trafficking victims are re-smuggled or even re-trafficked; that is, caught and deported but then re-recruited on their return home. Not all incidents of smuggling and trafficking include new victims – in some cases, the victimization is repeated over and over. Since we do not know the proportion of such cases, our ability accurately to gauge the number of new victims and the frequency of re-victimization suffers. Ko-lin Chin interviewed a young Chinese man held in a prison in Hong Kong for attempting to go to the United States illegally. Rather than being discouraged or deterred by his experience, the young man asked:

> Ask my sister to find a snakehead [Chinese trafficker] for me right away. Tell her to look for the best snakehead; don't worry about how much it's going to cost. Tell her I will be deported back to China after I've served my sentence here, and that means I should be back home by March 12. Tell her I want to stay at home for only a couple of days. Ask her to make sure whatever snakehead she finds is able to get me out of China by March 15. I must go to the United States.

Chin, (1999:164).

The number of trafficking cases and victims we know about is relatively small. But a variety of sources suggest there is good reason to suspect that what we see is only the tip of an iceberg, although we don't know how big the iceberg is. Many, perhaps most, cases do not come to the attention of any law enforcement authority and those that do may not be identified as trafficking cases. Clearly, estimates and numbers, so frequently cited and used as arguments for legislation, aid, funding, and so on, are not very reliable; yet any problem that is not perceived as being dramatically large is not likely to gain much attention. Therefore, it is in the best interests of both national and international organizations to promote often unreliable and overstated estimates.

I am not suggesting by any of this that human trafficking is not a problem: on the contrary, it is potentially a huge problem. What I am suggesting is that skepticism is needed when considering the magnitude and seriousness of the trafficking problem, and that there is clearly an urgent need for good, comprehensive, data and information. It is only on that basis that sound and effective policies to combat the problem can be developed.

Why human trafficking?

The business of trafficking in people represents the juxtaposition between human desires and needs, and market demands, entrepreneurial spirit, and unscrupulousness, which has fueled a variety of organized crime. While not drawing any conclusion about the question of whether human trafficking is totally, or even mainly, controlled by organized crime, it is useful to examine the supply and demand sides of the trafficking equation to see if there is anything to attract the attention of organized crime.

The push and pull factors I discussed earlier fall on both sides of that equation. Studies of universal influences on crime rates across countries by, among others, van Dijk and Kangaspunta (2000), reach conclusions that dovetail very well with these factors. Among the "motivational factors" they suggest influence crime are those such as a country's level of affluence, and a concept they call "strain;" the aggregate of people's reactions to not achieving their economic goals. Strain can be caused by unemployment, underemployment, or a significant dissatisfaction with income levels. Any of these could be push factors, driving the people affected to leave their homes and possibly their countries. Lack of, or limited, economic opportunity is a major push factor in human trafficking. My colleagues and I have heard this from young women trafficked from Ukraine, Moldova, and China.

Coupled with the motivational factors, according to van Dijk and Kangaspunta, are opportunity factors. Among these are those that enable or facilitate crime, such as weak social control. Weak or corrupt social control, including police, border patrol, customs agents, and immigration officials, creates opportunities for traffickers. This is also true in countries whose governing authorities fail to take human trafficking seriously. Because potential traffickers are affected by the level of economic opportunity in their country, in much the same fashion as their victims, they too are subject to this push factor. The traffickers' goal is the same as the victims – economic advancement – but their means are obviously different. Other opportunity factors for trafficking might include a country's geographical location and transport infrastructure. Airports and seaports facilitate the movement of people, as do road and rail systems, especially those that link with ports. This does not mean that countries that lack these characteristics and facilities are immune from human trafficking; it simply means that traffickers have to work somewhat harder to move their victims, and that therefore their prices will be higher.

Liang and Ye's (2001) description of emigration from the Fujian Province of China illustrates the interplay of motivational and opportunity factors. Fujian is on the coast of China, which, say Liang and Ye, makes the Fujianese particularly good candidates as "snake people:" that is, people engaged in human smuggling and trafficking. They are used to the sea and sea life, and ideally positioned. In addition, there is a sense of relative deprivation among the Fujianese. Relative deprivation is important, because poverty alone is not a primary motivation for crime, rather, it is the sense that some in a society have more, perhaps much more, than others. Those without feel themselves to be relatively deprived; they suffer from strain, and that can be a motivation to crime. This relative deprivation and strain arises in Fujian because some people are getting rich either by taking advantage of China's moves to create a market economy, or because they have family members living and working in the United States who remit large amounts of money to their relatives. The others, who remain at the bottom of the income ladder, see themselves as being deprived, and this can become a motivator for involvement in smuggling and trafficking.

According to O'Neill Richard (1999:3), the primary source countries for trafficking to the United States were Thailand, Vietnam, China, Mexico, Russia, Ukraine, and the Czech Republic. These countries have economic problems of varying degrees of severity – problems that lead to feelings of relative deprivation and strain – which are push factors for human smuggling and trafficking. O'Neill Richard quotes legal cases involving the trafficking of women into the United States that illustrate the pull side of the economic equation, and the involvement of unscrupulous employers. In one such case, involving Chinese women trafficked for sweatshop labor, such industry stalwarts as The Gap, The Dress Barn, Gymboree Corp., J.C. Penney, Lady Bryant, Nordstrom, Oshkosh B'Gosh, Sears Roebuck, Tommy Hilfiger and Wal-Mart were sued for exploitation (O'Neill Richard, 1999:50). Ukraine is a good example of "push." In Ukraine, it is estimated that sixty per cent of the unemployed are female, and that eighty per cent of those who have lost their jobs since Ukraine became independent from the Soviet Union in 1991 are women. The average urban salary is $30 a month, less in rural areas. The unfortunate result of these dire economic statistics is that the Ukrainian Ministry of the Interior estimates that 400,000 women have been trafficked since 1991; that Ukraine has become a major source of young women for the international sex market and is one of the largest suppliers of women for prostitution; Ukrainian women are the largest group of foreign women engaged in prostitution in Turkey; and that Ukrainian women are the second largest group of foreign women engaged in prostitution outside US military bases in Korea.

As I have indicated, other push factors include political repression, human rights abuses, and civil and military conflict. The former Yugoslavia, in particular Bosnia-Herzegovina and Kosovo, has been ravaged by civil war, ethnic cleansing, and military occupation. As a result, it has experienced a considerable amount of sex trafficking. Bosnia is unusual in also being a destination country for trafficking victims. That particular market may exist because of the relatively large numbers of unattached young men in the occupation and redevelopment forces – ready clients for sexual services.

The demand that fuels human trafficking is very much driven by the desire of people who want to migrate to seek work and a new life, but who are unable to do so by legitimate means. But demand also comes from employers who rely on undocumented labor, and from the clientele of the sex industry, as in Bosnia:

> [An] aspect critical to understanding the role of demand in this market is the willingness of many US employers to hire undocumented workers. For example, the illegal job market is flourishing in Florida and the INS estimates that about 350,000 illegal immigrants are currently living there. Some farms have earned the nickname, 'sweatshops in the sun' – as farmers and other business owners prefer illegal workers who don't complain and are willing to work for low wages. This is exacerbated by the fact that often migrants will accept jobs that no one else will ... In response to the need, some trafficking organizations have even begun to provide transportation directly to the work sites.
>
> Finckenauer and Schrock,
(www.ojp.usdoj.gov/nij/international/ht.html).

Changes in the global economy, including shifts in jobs and opportunity, and the collapse of previously closed societies, have added both to supply and the demand. David Kyle summed up these developments:

> The dislocating economic forces of globalization, which make workers, corporations, and states around the world compete as

never before, has produced both a glut of relatively ambitious migrants and the demand by employers for ever cheaper labor. When we add to this the combination of the fall of the Soviet Union, freeing hundreds of millions without adequate work, and an even greater number who live in fear of state or societal repression and persecution based on ethnicity, gender, or political activism, we begin to understand the enormous market for human smugglers and traffickers.

Kyle, (2003:2).

Human trafficking is made easier because many countries have weak, non-enforced, or non-existent laws against it. Some have very limited law enforcement capacity and lack expertise. For the most part, there is not enough coordination and cooperation between law enforcement agencies and across national borders in dealing with this transnational crime. A combination of factors and circumstances fuel the human trafficking business, including the normal human desire to improve one's circumstances, weak economies with few job opportunities, improved global transport and information systems, the low risk of prosecution in certain countries, corruption, and the predatory greed among employers and traffickers that feeds off the plight, hopes and dreams of others.

Who are the traffickers – organized crime or crime that is organized?

Knowing who the smugglers and traffickers are and how they operate should give us a sense of how organized human trafficking is, and to what extent it is truly a market and a business for organized crime.

Smugglers and traffickers transport people from one country to another by sea, land, and air. Some of their methods are quite sophisticated: they may use "people-carrying containers," pack people into containers with roses or Christmas trees to throw sniffer dogs, trained to detect people, off the scent, or smuggle migrants as replacement crews on ships, having provided them with fake identification documents. As evidence of the brutality of the business, in recent years there has been a number of incidents of smuggling and trafficking victims dying while being transported. They have been tossed into the sea and drowned, they have died of heat exhaustion and suffocation after being jam-packed into trucks, and they have died in overloaded ship containers not designed for human transport.

Smugglers' fees depend on local demand, the distances involved and the mode of transport. Migrants may pay from as little as several hundred dollars to as much as $75,000 to be smuggled to their destination; a fee which must entirely be paid beforehand. In the smuggling cases from China with which I am familiar, migrants raised the money to pay the fee from their families and friends. The obligation to repay is thus between the migrant and those who finance their migration. In contrast, in a trafficking case, the would-be migrant signs a contract and makes a payment to the trafficker. These contracts may include a clause stipulating that the traffickers can hold the migrants hostage until they or their families pay the remainder of the fee. At this point, the circumstances shift from migrant smuggling to human trafficking, and the migrants become trafficking victims. If, as is often the case, the entire fee is not immediately forthcoming, the victims are vulnerable to abuse and exploitation. For female victims, and especially children, this often means sexual exploitation. The crimes in which the traffickers are engaged thereby evolve from simply aiding and abetting illegal entry, to unlawful imprisonment, assault, and rape. Again, Kyle helps us understand how the trafficking business operates:

> Human traffickers often lure *en route* migrants away from their traveling companions, or – more commonly – pose as trusted migrant smugglers who simply want to help them find a job

abroad. Once the migrants arrive, however, they are made to pay rolling 'debts,' set by the traffickers with the threat of violence. Traffickers rely on intimidation, as well as the migrants' lack of state authorization or the cultural and linguistic skills necessary to seek help, to ensure the captivity of their victims.

Kyle, (2003).

Those who have examined the question of how trafficking is organized have concluded that "traffickers" are made up of a variety of individuals and groups from individual entrepreneurs, to small "mom and pop" operations, to sophisticated transnational criminal organizations, and permutations in between. How much of the human trafficking business is controlled by each of these types is impossible to say, given our current level of knowledge. What we can say is that, at a minimum, this must be a crime that is organized. An individual cannot carry it out, nor is it an impulse crime. There must, for example, be some person (or people) who finds and recruits the potential victims. In Taiwan, we were told about recruiters or "chicken heads" (young prostitutes or potential prostitutes are called chickens) who go to Chinese villages to recruit, entice, or coerce girls and young women to be trafficked back to Taiwan to work in the sex business. Once the victims have been recruited, transport must be arranged from source to destination. In the case of the Chinese women transported to Taiwan, they are typically moved by train or road vehicle to the Chinese coast, from where they are taken to Taiwan by boat across the Taiwan Strait. Someone meets the boats and moves the women to safe houses, then there is a further link to the sex club or brothel where the victims will be forced to work. This cannot be done without organization, but it does not necessarily require a sophisticated criminal organization.

In its report, *Trafficking in Persons: Global Patterns* (2006), the United Nations Office on Drugs and Crime concluded that there were two types of criminal groups involved in human trafficking.

The first type, which they called "hierarchical," has strong internal control and discipline, solid social or ethnic identity, and relies extensively on violence. Consistent with the earlier distinction between traditional organized crime and crimes that are organized, the UN indicated that these groups are not only engaged in human trafficking, but also in the transnational trafficking of various goods such as drugs and firearms, and in smuggling and kidnapping. The second type, which they called the "core" group, has limited numbers of individuals in a relatively tightly structured core, surrounded by a loose network of associates, seldom with strong social or ethnic identity. The core groups are strictly profit-oriented and opportunistic, and seem to shift between illegal activities, based on where the greatest profits can be made. They operate across national borders and are extremely violent. The suggestion seems to be that the organizers of human trafficking range from a few individual entrepreneurs who turn to it to meet the migration demand, up to and including sophisticated, perhaps transnational criminal organizations, which add trafficking to their existing criminal repertoires.

In their study of the sex trafficking of women in the United States, Raymond and Hughes (2001) interviewed victims, law enforcement personnel, social service providers, victims' advocates, and researchers. Asked about the businesses and networks instrumental in recruiting and controlling them, the victims cited businesses such as escort services, bars and brothels, and networks such as "biker gangs" and the Italian mafia. The majority of all the respondents, asked about possible involvement by organized crime groups, indicated that most trafficking organizations were small (one to five people), with only a few being large or very large (50–100 people) (Raymond and Hughes, 2001:48). Chin challenged the belief that human trafficking is currently controlled by organized crime. He concluded from his extensive research on Chinese smuggling and trafficking, "that the Chinese trade in human smuggling is not a form of organized crime but rather a

TRAFFICKERS OF WOMEN AND CHILDREN IN UKRAINE

Criminal groups appear to be responsible for carrying out the majority of the trafficking of women and children in Ukraine. These criminal groups are large and small, organized and unorganized, and national and international. Within these organizations, sixty percent (according to a sample survey) of the leaders are women, usually thirty to thirty-five years old; many are former prostitutes, but they may also be economists, teachers, and even lawyers. Typically, recruiters are fairly well educated, and must possess certain characteristics, to communicate effectively and be persuasive to gain some level of trust from their victims. In addition, the leaders of trafficking operations must locate and require a broad network of "helpers" or technical/logistical personnel. These helpers are recruiters, couriers, guides, guards, messenger drivers, or perform other tasks.

The role of the helper ends at the border crossing, when the "merchandise" is successfully transferred into the hands of pimps in exchange for a sum of money. Pimps can be either sex (sixty-two percent men, thirty-eight percent women). These pimps offer their "merchandise" to a predetermined and largely fixed clientele.

The accepting party (i.e., pimp or brothel owner) also may organize a special firm or enterprise for temporary job placement for the arriving women ... In Istanbul (Turkey), trafficked women work one or two weeks in retail sales before being given a minimum amount they must sell each day. When the women are unable to meet this minimum, debts are accumulated and they are forced to trade their bodies at night to pay off their debts. Alternatively, traffickers may initially contract with these women to work for a "dummy" company as a maid, waitress, or salesperson. Shortly after beginning such jobs, their employer forces them to sign a contract indicating their satisfaction with the company, which insulates the company from any future liability. In any case, women who would otherwise have freedom of mobility are forced by intimidation to service "clients" and participate in pornography and sex service industries.

Tatyana A. Denisova, (2004:48–49).

'business' controlled by many otherwise legitimate groups, both small and large, working independently, each with its own organization, connections, methods, and routes" (Chin, 1999:41). In their report on the commercial sexual exploitation of children, Estes and Weiner (2001) concluded that there are three types of traffickers in this particularly reprehensible crime: amateurs, small groups of organized criminals, and national and international trafficking networks (see Estes and Weiner, 2001, Exhibit 3.22). The latter were described as:

> Trafficking groups respond to the whole spectrum of needs of migrants, including the provision of fraudulent or genuine documents (stolen or altered) and the arrangement of accommodation and support in transit countries. One of the main characteristics of these networks is the flexibility in the reaction to new, unforeseen situations, because they have members located along the trafficking routes. The routes are often well-tested by other transnational criminal activities such as drug trafficking.

With respect to the potential for an increase in organized crime involvement, I see that involvement as very much related to demand and supply factors in the market, and to shifts in law enforcement and regulatory policies on migration. As we know from a variety of criminal markets, when demand for an illegal or regulated product or service remains the same (or increases), delivering this service continues to be (or becomes even more) lucrative and thus attractive to organized crime. In migration, the activities and services surrounding it are being made more difficult to deliver, because countries are making it more difficult to enter, either legally or illegally. Ironically, one of the unintended effects of crackdowns on illegal migration and the toughening of law enforcement against it may be to more widely open the door to organized crime. Increased costs (and thus profits) could attract more sophisticated criminal organizations, and increased risks and difficulties could drive out amateurs and the unorganized or poorly-organized. The end result will be that trafficking in people will become a greater part of the businesses of organized crime.

The role of corruption

As I pointed out in Chapter 1, corruption is an important defining characteristic of organized crime. The willingness and the ability to corrupt criminal justice officials and politicians enable criminal organizations to buy immunity from investigation, arrest, prosecution, or conviction. Members of organized crime are not the only ones who pay bribes or otherwise corrupt officials; thus the fact that human trafficking involves corruption – which it clearly does – is not a definitive indicator of its control by organized crime. However, organized crime groups are more likely to have the wealth and power that enhances their ability to corrupt more effectively. They can pay more, and they can reach higher into the law enforcement and political hierarchies.

Transnational human trafficking has some unique characteristics that require official corruption to play a particularly prominent role in its facilitation. Movement into and out of most countries is highly regulated and documented, and a host of government agents and agencies are responsible for monitoring and enforcing that regulation and documentation, including immigration officials, embassy and consular workers, border patrols, customs agents, and a variety of law enforcement officials. Successfully avoiding, or otherwise getting around, official requirements demands that traffickers employ corruption effectively. Officials in both destination and source countries may profit directly from pay-offs, and source countries may benefit from money sent home by migrants. In China, we saw expensive homes in otherwise poor villages, built with money sent home by husbands, fathers, and sons working in the United States – mostly in Chinese restaurants in New York City. There is an economic incentive for source countries (and their officials) to encourage their citizens to go abroad to work. This is not only true in China, but also in other countries, like Mexico. Much greater economic opportunity exists in the United States for people from China and Mexico than in their own countries. Therefore, officials not only do not want to discourage it, they want to facilitate it. And part of that facilitation may involve corruption.

In destination countries, one example of the money that corrupt individuals (in this case an attorney sworn to be an officer of the court) can make in human trafficking was reported by Kyle and Koslowski (2001:3). "[A] top New York immigration attorney, Robert Porges, was indicted [in 2000] on forty-four federal charges of helping up to seven thousand Chinese gain visas through fraudulent asylum claims, allegedly making over $13 million from the scheme." This case, those authors add, demonstrates the potential for corruption of individuals as well as of immigration policies. The Kyle and Koslowski book also describes corruption along the US/Mexican border which supports the argument that increased risks and profits may well lead to more organized crime involvement.

In their examination of human trafficking in Ukraine, Hughes and Denisova (2004) not only indict government and law enforcement officials in the corruption that is such a major part of the transnational political criminal nexus that operates the human trafficking business but also include the social or civil, sector of society. Civil society, which is present more or less in every country, includes a variety of NGOs, volunteer organizations, community groups, charities, churches, and faith-based groups.

I say that civil society is "more or less" present in various countries: the countries of the former Soviet Union are an unusual case of a weak civil society. Until 1991, the authoritarian Soviet government controlled every aspect of Soviet society. There was no viable civil society to speak of. When the Soviet Union broke apart and its components, such as Ukraine, became independent,

BORDER CORRUPTION

Border corruption has ... become a ... serious problem. Increased enforcement has increased the need for smugglers to bribe or buy entry documents from those doing the enforcing. And as smuggling groups have become more sophisticated and profitable – as a consequence of the higher demand and cost for their services and the heightened risks involved in providing those services – the capacity and means to corrupt have also grown. In one well-known case at the San Ysidro port of entry south of San Diego, US Customs inspector Guy Henry Kmett was arrested for helping a major smuggling ring move migrants through his inspection lane. The three vans busted in Kmett's lane carried Salvadorans, Guatemalans, Dominicans, and an Egyptian. Kmett came under suspicion after the Border Patrol noticed that the vans were parked at Kmett's house the day before. Kmett had spent about $100,000 in cash during the previous year on such items as a swimming pool, computers, and televisions. Law enforcement officials estimated that the Peraltas smuggling organization, which was trying to transport migrants through Kmett's lane, earned $1 million per month for smuggling one thousand migrants per month across the border.

On the Mexican side of the border, there have been numerous cases of official corruption involving migrant smuggling. In one high-profile case, the Mexican migration service's regional head in Tijuana, his deputy, and his chief inspector were all fired and charged with assisting the smuggling of non-Mexican migrants. The Tijuana office reportedly brought in as much as $70,000 weekly from the proceeds of migrant trafficking. It has also been reported that Tijuana police have taken bribes that amount to as much as $40,000 a month to permit the operation of safe houses where migrants stay before attempting to cross into the United States

Andreas, (2001:121).

there were no NGOs or community and volunteer organizations other than the government and the Communist Party. As the United States, other western countries, Japan, and entities like the

World Bank and the International Monetary Fund moved to support the development of democracy and freedom in the former Soviet states and in formerly communist Eastern Europe, one of their mechanisms was via NGOs. Their funding and other resources were funneled into different countries through NGOs but few, if any, NGOs then existed. Not to be dissuaded, the fledgling governments in those countries (which were mostly composed of reconstituted Communists) responded by creating NGOs to apply for and receive the substantial funds available. The result were oxymoronic "government-sponsored" NGOs, and the corruption described by Hughes and Denisova.

This history is important to understanding human trafficking, corruption, and organized crime because these countries of Eastern Europe and the former Soviet Union are the source of so much of the global traffic in women and children. Women, especially from Ukraine and the former Soviet republic of Moldova, are found in brothels, bars, sex clubs, and massage parlors around the world. The trafficking has, in no small part, been facilitated by corruption of the political-criminal-civil nexus. Hughes and Denisova conclude that the corruption that surrounds trafficking:

> ... thrives in environments where civil society is weak and the public institutions, in this case NGOs, are not accountable to their constituencies. When NGOs in sending [source] countries work to benefit destination countries instead of the women of their country, that is the corruption of civil society"
>
> Hughes and Denisova, (2004:85).

This means we can add the social agencies of civil society to our list of the possible beneficiaries of this sordid business.

Some examples

It will be helpful to examine a few actual cases to get a more detailed and in-depth look at the specifics of human smuggling and trafficking (who, how, what, and where), and perhaps a sense of just how organized the business is. Drawn from a roughly five-year period between 1998 and 2003, these cases describe a variety of victims and of types of victimization, and illustrate the practice of human trafficking in different regions of the world.

The first case was reported by the Transnational Crime and Corruption Center at American University, and dates from July 2000. Hundreds of young women from Paraguay were trafficked to the city of San Miguel in Argentina, allegedly for prostitution, although the women were originally told they would work as maids for families in San Miguel. The owner of the three brothels in Argentina that employed these women said he brought women from Paraguay because his clients were "demanding diversity." The women, many under eighteen years old, were essentially kept as slaves and said to be drugged most of the time. They were also kept under surveillance by security people, forbidden any contact with the outside world, and sometimes forced to service clients for fifteen hours at a time. The owner had bought these women in Paraguay for about US$300. His apparent rationale for the slave-like conditions was that not only had he "invested" the $300 purchase price, but also paid airfares and meal expenses. The women were working off this debt. If they tried to escape, another US$100 was added to their debt.

A team of investigators estimated the brothel owner's assets at over half a million dollars. A local newspaper stated that a hidden camera allegedly caught him paying bribes of up to US$18,000 to the local police and political figures in Argentina, in order to be permitted to operate his brothels. The owner further stated that the government also "sent their people," so he was also obliged to bribe officials in the executive, legislature and judiciary. He was ultimately apprehended, convicted and sentenced, and the women returned to Paraguay. However, skeptical victims' advocates did not believe he would serve his full sentence, because of the corruption that surrounded the case, and the involvement of local authorities in it (www.american.edu/traccc/Publications/ Phibes_StatusHTinLatinA.doc.).

Here we see the familiar combination of sexual exploitation, debt bondage and corruption. What we cannot tell from this report is how organized the activity was, nor whether it involved a "traditional" criminal organization and organized crime.

In her review of major trafficking cases in the US, O'Neill Richard (1999) described some prosecutions involving what she called "small or family crime rings." One was the case of US v. Cadena in 1998. From roughly February 1996 to March 1998, between twenty-five and forty Mexican women and girls (some just fourteen years old) were trafficked from Veracruz, Mexico to Florida and the Carolinas. Promised jobs as waitresses, housekeepers, or child and elder carers, they were instead forced to work as prostitutes, and endured assaults, rapes and forced abortions. Eventually, sixteen men were charged with a variety of crimes, including importing aliens for immoral purposes, involuntary servitude, visa fraud, and conspiracy. The ringleader, Rogerio Cadena, was convicted and sentenced to fifteen years in prison and ordered to pay $1 million in restitution. Seven others received sentences ranging from two and a half to six and a half years.

Raymond and Hughes (2001:100–105) catalogued incidents of trafficking to the United States between 1990 and 2000. They concluded that some of those cases displayed the characteristics of organized crime involvement. For example, in October 1999, the FBI arrested five alleged members of an Asian organized crime group in "Operation Bonsai." The group, which operated from South Florida, engaged in a variety of illicit activities, including transporting Asian women into the US, who they forced into prostitution to pay off their smuggling debts. In another 1999 case, US and Canadian law enforcement officials broke up an organized crime network that operated from Seattle and Toronto. Some three dozen Eastern Europeans were charged with drug trafficking, money laundering, and prostitution.

In these two cases, we see evidence of a criminal organization that has multiple criminal enterprises, and is operating transnationally. Finally, we can look at a 2003 case that was the largest trafficking case then prosecuted by the US.

Kil-soo Lee, a South Korean businessman, opened a business called Daewoosa Samoa Ltd., in Pago Pago, American Samoa in 1998. Daewoosa took over what was a struggling garment factory but instead of hiring local workers, Lee imported about 250 workers from Vietnam and another twenty-five from China to work there. The Vietnamese workers signed four-year contracts and paid about $5,000 each to cover the cost of their travel to American Samoa. Trouble began almost immediately after their arrival. First, the workers did not receive the pay promised, and eventually no pay at all. They were charged high fees for housing in sub-standard company dormitories and for extremely poor and inadequate food. Workers' passports were confiscated to prevent their escape, and when they protested, they were physically threatened and punished. Kil-soo Lee was aided in coercing and exploiting the factory workers by a representative of the Vietnamese agency that had originally recruited them, and by local American Samoan enforcers whom he hired for that purpose. This exploitation went on for several years. Finally, beginning in 2000 and lasting several years, Lee and Daewoosa were subject to a series of legal actions stemming from their harsh treatment of their employees. Lee was fined more than $350,000 by the Labor Department for failing to pay the workers. After the factory was shut down, he was arrested and sent to Hawaii for trial, at which he was convicted in 2003 for holding the workers in involuntary servitude. Daewoosa was ordered to pay $3.5 million in back pay and fines (Gittelsohn, 2003).

This case has the earmarks of a crime that is organized, but does not appear to involve organized crime. The traffickers were not engaged in other criminal activities, nor were they part of a criminal organization. Taken together, these cases tell us (although they are not a truly representative sample), that human trafficking can be carried out through a variety of mechanisms, only some of which might include organized crime. This does not make it any less of a problem; if anything, it complicates the challenges of coping with it.

Combating the problem

The US *Trafficking Victims Protection Act* of 2000 (TVPA) and the United Nations *Protocol on Trafficking in Persons* (2000) are examples of significant recent efforts to combat the human trafficking problem. The UN protocol is intended to prevent and combat trafficking in people, assist trafficking victims, and promote co-operation among the member countries to accomplishing those purposes. Cooperation is especially important, in light of the transnational nature of the problem; countries cannot combat transnational crime problems alone. The TVPA employs a three-tiered approach including prevention, prosecution, and protection. It is intended to increase criminal sanctions for trafficking (for example, twenty years' imprisonment for selling someone into slavery), and to improve both laws, and law enforcement, against trafficking. The TVPA makes trafficking victims eligible for the Federal Witness Security Program (which I shall describe in a later chapter).

A companion law to the TVPA is the Immigration and Nationality Act (18 U.S.C. 1590 2003). This law provides for the granting of a T visa to trafficking victims, which allows them temporary residence in the United States. To be eligible for this visa, victims must, among other things, comply with requests for help in the investigation or prosecution of traffickers. This is very important because while the victims best know who the traffickers are and exactly what was done to victimize them, they are reluctant to cooperate in investigations or testify for fear of retaliation against them and their families. As in other forms of organized crime, people with critical knowledge must be given incentives and protection to encourage them to share it with investigators and prosecutors.

As well as improving law enforcement and prosecution, it is important to remember if efforts to combat organized crime are to be successful, another part of the puzzle must also be solved. There is always a demand side to the equation – and organized crime responds to demands for goods and services that are illegal or unavailable. In this case, the demand is for men, women, and children who will be exploited and victimized. A number of what the US State Department describes in its Trafficking in Persons Report as "best practices" have been undertaken (see www.state.gov/documents/organization/21555.pdf). Among the more interesting, South Korea has closed brothels employing trafficking victims, and threatened to publish the names of brothel owners and patrons; the United Arab Emirates is enforcing a ban on the use of underage, underweight camel jockeys, to prevent children being brought illegally into the country to ride racing camels; the government of Mozambique has joined with various organizations to sponsor festivals, nationwide youth debates, dances, dramas, and posters to increase public awareness of child prostitution; and African governments, the International Labor Organization, and the Federation for International Football Associations has teamed up with airlines, popular soccer players, music personalities, and television and radio stations throughout Africa to conduct a continent-wide anti-child labor campaign during the Africa Cup of Nations Soccer tournament.

The kit to combat human trafficking must contain a variety of tools, including outlawing human trafficking and its ancillary activities, strengthening the capacity of law enforcement agencies to investigate and prosecute these crimes, increasing criminal sanctions, cracking down on corruption, providing services for victims, and expanding the use of witness protection programs.

Ultimately, however, an enormously ambitious economic development effort will be needed, to reduce the disparities between the "have" and "have not" nations, and between the source and destination countries. It is those disparities that drive men, women, and children to seek economic opportunities in other countries, and thus to become vulnerable to being victimized by traffickers, including those traffickers sophisticated enough and organized enough to be regarded as being "true" organized crime.

7

Confronting the enemy

I hope it has become clear that organized crime has certain distinctive and unique characteristics that both shape how we attempt to combat gangsters and their criminal enterprises and greatly affect our success in doing so. The first and foremost of these defining characteristics is the use, and the reputation for use, of extreme violence. Violence makes criminal ventures such as extortion, protection rackets, loan sharking, and "pump and dump schemes" successful. Violence intimidates victims, witnesses, and potential jurors in criminal trials; they fear for their lives and the lives of their loved ones. Violence means that people with knowledge, including direct knowledge, of mob crimes keep quiet, which severely hampers the ability of law enforcement officers to get the evidence and information they need successfully to prosecute the criminals.

A second characteristic is the clandestine nature of much organized crime activity. In "regular" or unorganized crime, an individual (or group of individuals) commits a crime against a single victim at a particular place and time. The police may observe it, someone may see what is going on and report it, or the police may conduct an investigation to find the offender. Although the police are not always successful, the common criminal runs the risk of getting caught. This is not the way organized crime works. There, the criminals at risk of being observed and reported are usually only the lowest-level offenders, at the bottom of the criminal pyramid. The others higher up in the pyramid, who orchestrate and profit from the crime, are buffered or hidden from the risk of getting caught. They cannot, at least not easily, be linked to specific crimes.

The third, important, distinguishing characteristic – one that I have returned to throughout this book – is that organized crime provides illegal goods and services that are in demand. People are not generally in favor of houses being broken into, cars stolen, women being raped, and other criminality, but they do (or enough do) want to gamble, buy drugs, and use prostitutes. This greatly affects our ability and success in preventing and controlling these, and other, problems. Defined as so-called "victimless" crimes, the parties and consumers involved do not report their involvement, for obvious reasons. The result of these factors is that organized crime has become an employer of last (or perhaps first, depending on individual circumstances and choices) resort in many places. Involvement with a criminal organization provides income and economic opportunities where non-criminal employment is either not available or not lucrative enough to compete with criminal opportunities. This may well prove the most intractable factor in efforts at prevention and control.

Before we look at how these characteristics affect the methods and tools that are used to pursue criminal organizations, let me say a few words about where I think the responsibilities for combating them lie. In the "two wheels of a cart" analogy, one of the wheels represented government; to further the analogy, consider that there are actually two elements – spokes and a rim – to a wheel. At the highest levels of government – policy making and strategy – there are responsibilities to make fighting organized crime a priority, to expose crimes and criminals through hearings and special investigations, to pass the laws that will give law enforcement and prosecution agencies the weapons they need for the fight, to provide the critical resources and personnel crime fighters need, and to take a strong stand against corruption by and collusion with organized crime. Encouraging and facilitating operations are also important government responsibilities, as is facilitating economic and human development. Within the criminal justice and legal systems, police, prosecutors, and judges must aggressively, within the bounds of the rule of law, seek out, prosecute, convict, and sentence gangsters. They must use the tools given to them by law and policy judiciously. And because corruption is one of the major policies of organized crime, criminal justice officials must resist and root out corruption in their own ranks.

The second wheel of the cart represents civil society. The people, both singularly and jointly, must resist and combat gangsters and mobsters at all levels. This means that people have to urge their representatives in government to create the tools, and provide the necessary resources, for the war on organized crime. They must support law enforcement efforts; refuse to buy illegal goods and services, such as drugs and stolen goods; not pay bribes; participate in local efforts, such as those in Sicily, to prevent and control organized crime; and they must push for, and participate in, human development efforts that help destroy the roots of organized crime. None of this is easy. The need for citizen and community participation and economic development has fallen most short; not surprisingly, for they are by far the most difficult to achieve.

Let us look at some common ways to combat the scourge of organized crime, paying particular attention to how they are shaped by organized crime's character, where the responsibility for implementing particular approaches lies, and to the pros and cons of their use. Much of the following discussion is based on my experience with, and knowledge of, policies and practices in the United States. However, the ratifying of the UN *Convention Against Transnational Organized Crime* and other international efforts means many other countries have adopted, and are now using, these methods.

The anti-organized crime tool-kit

• *Criminal intelligence*: one of the essential requirements for law enforcement is good information. This information is referred to as "intelligence" and more specifically as "criminal intelligence." The building blocks of legal cases against organized crime figures are bits of information, of intelligence, usually built piece by piece, slowly, painstakingly, over long periods of time.

When I worked with the New York State Organized Crime Task Force in their investigation of Russian émigré organized crime in the northeastern United States in the mid-1990s, investigators spent many hours in surveillance. Starting with one or more suspect individuals, often based on a tip from another law enforcement agency or an informant, they would try to find out all they could about the suspect's social habits. Who socialized with whom? License plate numbers from cars parked at a wedding or bar mitzvah that the suspect attended would identify the other attendees. Phone surveillance systems (pen registers) traced all the numbers called from the suspect's phone. Any criminal record the suspect might have anywhere, was checked, as well as those of any criminal associates who might have been involved. Sometimes they sought financial records. They scanned newspapers for any mention of the target individual and any others who might be linked to them. And so on.

This highly labor-intensive effort was for the simple purpose of learning as much about the individual as possible, to determine if he or she were involved in criminal activities, and if so, who else might be involved. This sort of information is usually not evidence: attending a bar mitzvah is not a crime, nor is calling someone on the phone. Its purpose is to establish whether or not there is enough smoke to be concerned about a fire. There may be sufficient reason to nurture an informant within the group or insert an undercover investigator, or there may be cause to seek a warrant for electronic surveillance. Intelligence is a step toward evidence but, with rare exceptions, is not itself evidence. Sometimes surveillance proves to be a dry well and never proceeds.

The need for intelligence collection arises from the covert nature of organized crime. It is a way of discovering who the hidden figures, further up in the criminal pyramid, might be and what they might be up to. If law enforcement agencies share their intelligence (unfortunately too often not the case), they may be able to get a good picture of what is going on; and then they have a basis for action. As more and more instances of transnational organized crime occur, the sharing of intelligence information becomes ever more important, but at the same time more problematical. Investigators are reluctant to share information with counterparts in countries where there is a great deal of corruption, where organized crime has a cozy relationship with government agencies, or where the roles of police and national security personnel overlap.

In the face of the benefits, the main down-side of intelligence gathering is its potential for invasion of privacy. People totally innocent of any crime may have their social habits and telephone conversations monitored by government agents. There is also the danger of guilt by association: attending a wedding also attended by Al Capone or John Gotti does not mean you are a member of their crime family. As with just about every tool in the tool-kit, the question of whether the end justifies the means must be considered. Careful auditing and supervision by law enforcement managers and legal advisors is needed, to insure that abuses do not occur.

- *Electronic surveillance*: if there is a sufficient basis for proceeding further in a criminal investigation – specifically, under US law, having "probable cause" – the investigators may ask a judge to issue a warrant to eavesdrop on a suspect or tap their telephone. Eavesdropping may involve planting a listening device – a "bug" – in a suspect's home, or office or car, or by having an informant or undercover agent wear a device which picks up and records conversations.

In a criminal trial, these recordings carry enormous weight with a jury when they hear a defendant's voice discussing their crimes. This sort of evidence can be the key to or only link between "Mr. Big" and any criminal activity. It is a useful tool, and sometimes the only one which can penetrate the cocoon in which the bosses operate.

But even more than with general intelligence-gathering, electronic surveillance offers considerable potential for abuses of the right to privacy. A lightning rod for controversy in today's war on terrorism, the power of government to penetrate the inner sanctum of our private lives has been much debated and much abused. Do government agents listen in every time you order a pizza, make an appointment, or arrange a play date for your child? The law requires that such irrelevant conversations are not monitored, and probably most law enforcement agents obey that law. But there is, nevertheless, the opportunity for abuse. Citizens of countries with a history of totalitarian practices are especially wary of electronic surveillance. It is a powerful tool, but one to be used only with extreme care.

- *Informants and undercover operations*: because of the surreptitious nature of criminal organizations and their activities, surreptitious methods are needed to combat them – akin to fighting fire with fire. Criminal organizations may be penetrated directly, by people, as well as, and sometimes in conjunction with, electronic listening devices planted. These human penetrators – some call them brave but others offer much less flattering labels – are of two kinds: informants and undercover agents.

Informants are, generally, a very mixed bag both in terms of who they are and in their effectiveness. Why would anyone risk life and limb to become a "rat," or "stool pigeon"? There are several reasons. A typical technique of law enforcement agencies is to catch the "little fish" – those at or near the bottom of the pyramid who are the most exposed to getting caught – and use them as bait to catch the "bigger fish." This can mean many things, but one is turning them into informants. Targets, or suspects, agree to cooperate with investigators in return for more lenient treatment. Because they are insiders, already part of the criminal group, they can gain invaluable information. Another reason a person might become an informant is for money: investigators pay for information. In rare cases, they may simply be Good Samaritans. Paid informants may or may not be criminals, but the most useful generally are.

To provide valuable information, informants obviously must have access to the inner workings of a criminal group. As with electronic surveillance, informants can provide the critical information that enables the conviction of the top people. However, there are a number of risks involved in relying on them. Because most of these informants are themselves criminals – "low lifes" as defense attorneys often refer to them – their information can be very suspect. They are not known for honesty and integrity and their information is obviously self-serving.

There have been instances where the relationship between an informant and their law enforcement handlers has become too cozy. Informants have used their protected status as a license to rob and even murder. In one of the most infamous examples in US law enforcement history, James "Whitey" Bulger, head of an Irish-American crime ring in Boston, collaborated with Boston FBI agents supposedly to provide them with information about the Italian Mafia. These agents shielded Bulger from being investigated and prosecuted for a variety of serious crimes, including assault, hijackings, bank hold-ups, and murder. Bulger collaborated with the agents, to their mutual benefit, but the great detriment of the community, innocent victims, and the overall integrity of the FBI. Dick Lehr and Gerard O'Neill aptly titled their book that tells this sordid tale: *Black Mass – the Irish Mob, the FBI, and a Devil's Deal* (Lehr & O'Neill, 2000).

Undercover investigators are law enforcement agents who penetrate criminal organizations. They must be a member of the organization while collecting the information that can be used to bring it down. This is obviously risky. The undercover agent has to wear several hats: they must hang out with the gangsters; drink and socialize with them. They may have to participate in planning crimes, but somehow avoid committing any. They must prepare reports and feed back any information obtained to their colleagues and superiors. And they must maintain some semblance of a family life while keeping their criminal cronies from learning anything about their real private life. Accomplishing all of these things is no mean feat. The book *Donnie Brasco* tells the story of how one FBI agent juggled these hats while working as an undercover investigator. From the book, and the later film, we get a sense of the toll on him and his family, and ultimately on his career in law enforcement.

A related kind of undercover law enforcement tool is a "sting" operation. With their knowledge of how criminal markets operate, investigators set up targets to bait gangsters. In the investigation of Russian émigré organized crime to which I have referred, investigators learned that small businesses in Brighton Beach, Brooklyn were vulnerable to extortion and protection rackets. To attract, and hopefully catch, the criminals who were victimizing these businesses, investigators set up their own business; they rented a store space and opened a small business selling medical supplies. Despite months of operation and exposure to risk, there were no approaches from any extortionists; no one attempted to "put the arm" on the operators. The investigators suspected that this might have been because the owner of the building in which they rented space may have become suspicious and passed the word to stay away from this particular business. Not withstanding this failure, sting operations have been used successfully against organized crime. The greatest caution to be exercised in their use – apart from physical danger – is for investigators not to cross the line into entrapment. Providing an opportunity for criminals to commit crimes is legally acceptable, but entrapment – enticing them, by planting the idea of criminality where it may not have existed before, is not.

- *Grants of immunity*: beyond the squeezing of the little fish by threatening harsh punishment, law enforcement agencies can also gain their cooperation by offering immunity from criminal prosecution. Because the people with the most valuable information about criminal organizations and activities are themselves criminals, they are liable to prosecution once caught. To gain their cooperation, perhaps by giving testimony, they are offered limited immunity. This is an example of a clash between a fundamental right – the right not to incriminate oneself – and the need of a government for critical information with which successfully to prosecute organized crime.

In US practice, grants of immunity come in two forms: use and transactional. The US Constitution protects individuals from incriminating themselves, so transactional and use immunity are granted to preserve this constitutional protection. Transactional immunity is broad (sometimes referred to as an "immunity bath"), but a witness given the more limited "use immunity" may still be prosecuted on evidence not gathered from the protected testimony.

The value of grants of immunity as a law enforcement tool is now recognized internationally. Article 26 (3) of the UN Convention Against Transnational Organized Crime encourages all countries to consider "granting immunity from prosecution to a person who provides substantial cooperation in the investigation or prosecution of an offence covered by this Convention."

• *Witness protection*: the propensity of criminal organizations to use violence has long meant that knowledgeable witnesses have been reluctant to come forward to testify against mobsters. To overcome this fear, US officials decided that something substantial had to be done to protect them, not only during the trial and its aftermath, but forever. The Witness Protection Program, created as part of the Organized Crime Control Act of 1970, was their response.

Unlike grants of immunity, potentially valuable witnesses are not necessarily criminals, although many are. Formal witness protection programs are a considerable commitment. The government gives the witness a new identity, sets them up in a new location with a new job, and includes their family. In the history of the program in the United States, roughly 8,000 witnesses – mostly criminals – and 10,000 family members have been given new identities. The program costs US taxpayers $50 million a year; the conviction rate in the cases in which those 8,000 witnesses testified is said to be around ninety per cent.

Many other countries are now considering, or already have, witness protection laws similar to US law. Serbia, Bosnia-Herzegovina, Montenegro, Latvia, Lithuania, Poland, the Czech Republic, Slovakia, Australia, and Canada are among the countries currently providing security for witnesses,

Figure 7 The aftermath of the Sicilian Mafia's car bomb assassination of anti-Mafia judge Giovanni Falcone in Palermo, Sicily, May 24, 1992. In addition to Judge Falcone, the explosion killed Falcone's wife and three policemen who were escorting the couple to their home (AP Photo).

mainly in organized crime and war crimes trials. The smaller countries sometimes find it necessary to relocate witnesses to other countries to protect them. Wherever they exist, their goal is similar; to insure that a witness can provide key testimony without being harmed or intimidated.

One of the best-known and most effective of the witness programs is that of Italy. In the 1990's, particularly during the anti-mafia campaign that followed the mafia assassinations of Judges Falcone and Borsellino, thousands of organized crime defectors came into the witness protection program. Known as *pentiti* (repentants), they provided invaluable information and evidence that not only led to a much better understanding of the operations of the mafia, but also to numerous convictions of mafia figures (see Letizia Paoli's *Mafia Brotherhoods* (OUP, 2003) for an excellent account of this history).

Although witness protection programs have been generally successful, there have been at least two drawbacks. As with the other tools, there are "cons" along with the "pros." Some organized crime figures who become protected witnesses have been accustomed to big city living, with all that entails. They find the rural or suburban locations to which they are relocated boring and unsatisfying. They are isolated from friends and family, except those who have moved with them. And they are expected to maintain a regular job; something many have never done in their lives. On top of that, most of these criminals fully enjoyed their lives of crime. Consequently, some protected witnesses opt out of the protection program, as is their right. And some of those have ended up dead.

In a recent, high-profile, case in the US, federal prosecutors granted leniency and witness protection to Sammy "The Bull" Gravano, former under-boss of the Gambino crime family, in return for his testimony against John Gotti, godfather of the Gambinos. Gotti was convicted mainly on the strength of Gravano's cooperation with the government and the evidence he provided. Later, Sammy became bored with his protected, but dull, life on the right side of the law, and decided to "come out of the closet" of witness protection. Sammy did not try to lay low, as might have been expected (a contract had been put out on his life) but was brazen in his visibility: for example, he made little attempt to change his appearance for a series of television interviews. Eventually, he went back to his life of crime, and he and others were subsequently convicted of drug dealing and sent to prison.

The Gravano case illustrates a second problem that can arise with witness protection: many of these people are career criminals. They may continue their criminal lives while in the witness protection program, creating an intolerable situation for their government minders. There have been other cases where people in the witness protection program have been prosecuted for new crimes.

• RICO: as I described briefly in the first chapter, by far the most powerful tool that US prosecutors can employ against organized crime is the *Racketeer-Influenced and Corrupt Organizations* (RICO) law. Like the legal provision for witness protection, RICO was included in the 1970 Organized Crime Control Act. To date, this approach to combating organized crime is more or less confined to the United States.

RICO rests on the assumption that organized crime is an enterprise; a business of some kind. The original purpose of the law was to combat the infiltration of legitimate business enterprises by organized crime, being largely a response to a number of instances in which mobsters had taken over labor unions. By enterprises, the law means whatever business organized crime can infiltrate – it could be a legal business, a labor union, or a government agency. A subsequent court decision extended the meaning of enterprise explicitly to include an organized crime family (see US v Turkette, 452 US 576, 583, 1981).

One of the unique features of RICO is that it treats as a single offense the operation of the particular enterprise, through a "pattern of racketeering activity." This is defined as "criminal acts that have similar purposes, results, participants, victims, or methods of commission, or that are otherwise interrelated."

What establishes that the enterprise is being operated as a racketeering enterprise is the commission of two "predicate acts" within ten years. Under US statutes, predicate acts comprise the serious crimes in federal and state statutes. This is how the links between people and crimes are established. Thus, the net for catching criminals is very wide. In response to the character of organized crime, the law covers violence, the provision of illegal goods and services, corruption in either labor or management, corruption in government, and criminal fraud.

The linking of predicate acts over time and between people enables prosecutors to bring charges against people who have no other direct connection to a particular crime. Prosecutors are able to penetrate the buffer protecting those high in the criminal hierarchy, and to bring charges against all the members of a criminal enterprise at the same time.

RICO provides a wide range of criminal and civil sanctions, including imprisonment for life where the predicate offense is punishable with a life sentence, and the forfeit of assets gained through the operation of the racketeering enterprise. This mandatory forfeit includes any criminal profits used to acquire the enterprise, and any interest obtained as a result of fraud or extortion. Convicted criminals are liable to lose houses, apartments, cars, boats, jewelry, properties, and more – forfeits that can amount to millions of dollars. The law also allows victims to sue offenders for damages suffered as a result of the enterprise.

As a result of these severe penalties, mob figures can be, and have been, more readily convinced to cooperate in the prosecution of fellow mobsters. The alternative, if convicted, is to spend the rest of their lives in prison and lose all their financial assets, which affects not only them but their families. Among its other results, RICO has enabled prosecutors to crack the protective cover of *omerta*.

Many US prosecutors and other public officials consider RICO to be the single most effective tool in prosecuting systematic organized criminal activity, but it has its criticisms and controversies, which explains why other countries have been reluctant to adopt RICO-like laws and procedures. Among the criticisms is the charge of "vagueness," which stems from the failure of the statute to define either organized crime or racketeering. This absence of definition means prosecutors have used (some say abused) RICO to go after alleged "criminal" enterprises far removed from organized crime, including political groups and operators of abortion clinics. The possibility of having the label "racketeer" attached to them has forced some plaintiffs not involved in organized crime into making what critics consider extortionate settlements in cases that may truly be without merit. When certain mob-infiltrated labor unions in the US were successfully prosecuted as racketeering enterprises, innocent union members, who may already have been victimized by the mob infiltration of their union, were subsequently "re-victimized" by the government through having to forfeit their pension funds. This is an example of the very broad-brush treatment that the law allows. A final example is that RICO violates protections against "double jeopardy:" critics charge that in citing a predicate offense that may be ten years old, the law permits defendants to be re-prosecuted for crimes of which they had already been convicted and for which they may have completed their sentences. The Racketeer Influenced and Corrupt Organizations act is a prime example of the dilemma posed by the question of whether the ends justify the means. RICO has clearly been very effective in combating organized crime, but at what many consider to be an enormous cost. So far, the official US answer to the ends/means question has been yes, but other countries have not chosen to follow its lead.

International efforts against organized crime

As I have indicated, the globalization of organized crime means there is a greater need than ever before for uniformity of laws, procedures and law enforcement practices among nations. One very important step was the UN Convention on Transnational Organized Crime approved in Palermo, Sicily in 2000. (For an overview and summary see *Trends in Organized Crime*, Summer

2000, Vol. 5, No. 4.) It was no accident that Palermo (a power center of the Sicilian Mafia) was selected as the site for the signing ceremony.

The Convention, which has since been ratified by the necessary number of countries and become an international treaty, specifies a number of "organized crimes" that are commonly transnational. These crimes are: participation in organized criminal groups, money laundering, corruption, and the obstruction of justice. There are also two protocols to the Convention that criminalize human trafficking and human smuggling. When a country ratifies the Convention, it is obliged to incorporate these crimes into its own criminal code, making them criminal offenses in each ratifying country. The same is true of the criminal procedures in the Convention for improving cooperation on extradition, mutual legal assistance, the transfer of criminal proceedings, and joint investigations. Given countries' vastly different legal traditions, law enforcement philosophies, and attitudes toward punishment and their differing degrees of tolerance for, and the presence of, corruption, it may be difficult to achieve cooperation and coordination. This will affect the collection and exchange of information, the tracing of firearms linked to crime, and especially the identification of foreign nationals suspected of trafficking, smuggling, or being organized criminals. Nevertheless, the creation of the Convention is a great step forward.

Other steps toward international collaboration include the creation in 1989 of the Financial Action Task Force on Money Laundering (FATF). The governments of the G-7 group of industrialized countries, twenty-six other countries and two regional organizations established FATF as an intergovernmental body, to develop and promote policies to combat money laundering. Other international groups, such as the Organization of American States and the Organization of Economic Cooperation and Development, have also worked to create an international response to common criminal threats. The United Nations, as well as pushing for the Convention on Transnational Crime, has also established the United Nations Office for Drug Control and Crime Prevention, consisting of the United Nations International Drug Control Program and the Center for International Crime Prevention.

The international nature of organized crime has promoted other efforts by governments and various criminal justice agencies to form partnerships that cross national borders. The International Criminal Police Organization (Interpol), with a membership of 177 countries, is the largest international law enforcement partnership in the world. Interpol's goal is to provide "an efficient, secure and reliable telecommunications system that links each of the Interpol National Central Bureaus by email and gives automated access to a central database of information on international crime and criminals" (Kendall, 1998). The value of Interpol is that law enforcement authorities who are looking for a criminal suspect can query the database to learn whether any other countries have any information on this suspect, possibly including his or her whereabouts. European countries have created a counterpart to Interpol: Europol. Europol is a multi-national enforcement agency dedicated to increasing transborder enforcement and intelligence partnerships across European countries. It too is intended to bridge differing languages, legal systems, cultures, and crime problems.

Legalizing or decriminalizing the activities of organized crime

Organized crime makes significant profits from providing goods and services that are illegal. Some experts argue that because people obviously want to buy these things, we should consider making them available legally, so as to take the profit out of the hands of criminals. There are two ways of doing this: legalization and decriminalization. Legalization is the preferred approach of those who advocate legal reforms. It means making an activity or aspects of an activity legal, while keeping it subject to certain government regulation. Selling alcohol and cigarettes are examples of legal but regulated activities. These sales are restricted by licensing requirements and age limits, violations of which can result in loss of license and possible criminal penalties. The less-popular approach to changing a society's posture toward illicit goods and services is decriminalization. This means removing all criminal sanctions and allowing people to buy goods or services, or engage in what activities they wish. A number of arguments have been put both for and against the less–controversial alternative, legalization:

- For

    Laws which criminalize goods and services for which there is a large and continuing public demand should be changed. Meeting these kinds of demands currently requires the organization, criminal sophistication and capital investment that only criminal organizations possess. Present laws do not eliminate the demand but do create a lucrative market for organized crime. Changing them would deprive organized crime of this market.

    The enormous profits of organized crime often come from providing illicit goods and services that are not seen as particular harmful by many in society. However, these profits are used to finance other illegal activities viewed as much more clearly detrimental to the public interest. Legalizing less-harmful activities would, it is believed, take resources away from those that are more harmful. If gambling were legalized, it might take away some of the impetus for loan sharking and its attendant violence.

    Many of the current laws against drugs, gambling, prostitution, and so on, are unenforceable. This inevitably leads to the corruption of the police and other criminal justice agents.

Shifting emphasis from what are regarded as generally ineffective enforcement attempts against low-level vice operatives under the current law, to a more concerted attack on the upper echelons of criminal organizations would be a much more effective strategy to combat organized crime in the long run.

• Against

Legalization (and decriminalization) would allow organized crime to continue to engage in "victimless" crimes, but on a legal basis. Any regulatory restrictions placed on drugs, gambling, or prostitution would continue to create incentives for some to avoid those restrictions.

Because legalization involves licensing and regulation, there would continue to be many opportunities for corruption and so legalization would not be the answer to public corruption. Legal ways of providing formerly outlawed goods and services would not be able to compete with the services and advantages that organized crime can offer. The illegal numbers racket survives despite government-sanctioned lotteries; the skills, expertise, experience, contacts, capital, and flexibility of criminal organizations would enable them still to dominate the market. The question of legalizing the sorts of activities and behaviors that organized crime routinely supplies is very thorny. Some countries, for example, the Netherlands, have adopted a policy of allowing limited personal possession and use of "soft" drugs, but most other countries continue to criminalize this. Likewise, some countries permit controlled prostitution, and some have legalized various forms of gambling. The policy debates revolve around moral, legal, and practical issues, and thus usually result in sharply divided public opinion and political support. It is very hard to see if there will ever be a time when legalization of the kinds of goods and services we have been talking about will become a major weapon in the global fight against organized crime.

Rooting out organized crime

For the most part, approaches to combating organized crime are reactive. They rely heavily on the law and on law enforcement. A number of steps could be taken (and some are already being taken) to improve law enforcement policy, ranging from better policies and training in the use of informants and better controls of the use of asset forfeiture, to improved law enforcement cooperation across national boundaries, including exchange of intelligence, mutual legal assistance, assignment of specialized personnel to fighting organized crime, and coordination of national and international laws. However, international police cooperation remains very spotty and hit-and-miss. Ironically, transnational criminals are often much more adept at operating on the global scene than are the police. Beyond the improvements needed in law enforcement is a critical need to strengthen immigration policies in source, transit and destination countries in screening for trafficking victims, illegal migrants, and criminals. It would also be desirable to link financial aid and technical assistance from donor countries and organizations to aggressive measures against corruption in recipient countries.

Without deprecating the necessity of these types of efforts, or failing to acknowledge the successes achieved, focussing exclusively or even mostly on such methods is to concentrate only on one wheel of the cart. As long as the economic, social and political conditions that fertilize organized criminality exist, so will organized crime. Absence of economic opportunity and poverty in too many countries leads their people to look to criminal organizations as their way out: organized crime is their route to success. The business of producing, trafficking, and marketing drugs is a primary example. It motivates farmers in Afghanistan, Colombia, and Mexico to grow poppies, coca and marijuana. It provides well-paid jobs for young men, many of whom may lack education and skills. It motivates "mules," mostly young women, to transport drugs, hidden in balloons which they swallow and later excrete. Most of, if not all, these poor people are not criminals, and if there were suitable alternatives, would not choose to engage in crime. Poor economic conditions make girls and young women vulnerable to human traffickers. They see bleak prospects, few jobs, and little advancement and thus succumb to the promise of "opportunity." In some cases, they continue to do so even after a taste of what that "opportunity" really means. Would they do this if they did not feel they had to? The same can be said of the poor families who sell their children to human traffickers. Other things being equal, would they choose to do this? And what of those involved in the harvesting and trafficking of human organs?

Corruption and a weak commitment to the rule of law also tend to be characteristic of undeveloped countries and both correlate with the presence of organized crime. Corruption arises from political appointments based on connections rather than merit and from low-paying government jobs that nevertheless provide numerous opportunities for graft. Well-paid, and professional, civil servants cost money. Some of the most convincing statistical data attesting to the relation of organized crime to human development and the rule of law comes from an as yet unpublished UN report. The countries with the most robust rule of law (defined as independent and professional prosecutors and judges) had the lowest levels of organized crime and vice versa. The same, by the way, was true of terrorism. Likewise, higher levels of organized crime were highly correlated with low levels of human development (using a comparative measure of poverty, literacy, education and life expectancy). Even stronger was the tie between *per capita* gross domestic product (GDP) and organized crime – higher GDP is associated with lower organized crime. Recalling the earlier discussion of crime, opportunity and choice as explaining organized crime, these data clearly tell us that, although there is certainly choice being exercised, that choice is very much constrained and shaped by the circumstances in which people find themselves. Changing those circumstances will be an enormous challenge for the global community.

I end with the wise words of Pogo, with which I began. "We have met the enemy, and he is us!" Human needs, human weaknesses, and plain old human greed may prove to be the most intractable problems in combating organized crime and the mafia.

Appendix:
books and films

Attempting to list the books and other media that have organized crime or mafia as their subject matter is practically impossible and even if it were not, it would not be especially useful and informative. While necessarily subjective, let me offer some of what I regard as the more prominent non-fiction books and films on the subject. Television coverage, with one or two exceptions, is often too ephemeral to be meaningful and video games and rap music are among the newest cultural forms exploiting this subject; therefore any consideration of their message and impact must be preliminary.

Even the more serious informational media have not been immune to the mafia focus. The principal subject of major non-fiction books on organized crime in the United States has been the American LCN. The most groundbreaking include Cressey's *Theft of the Nation* (1969), Albini's *American Mafia: Genesis of a Legend* (1971), Ianni's *A Family Business: Kinship and Social Control in Organized Crime* (1972), *The Mafia Mystique* by Dwight Smith (1975), and Anderson's *The Business of Organized Crime* (1979). While considering the subject from different angles, these books provided a deep understanding of organized crime, or at least of a particular brand of it. But I suspect that the enlightenment gained from them has been limited to serious students of the topic.

Two later, less scholarly, but more popular books dealing with LCN have been especially influential because each was the basis for a major motion picture. Nicholas Pileggi's *Wise Guy: Life in a*

Figure 9 Actor Al Pacino is seen as Michael Corleone in a scene from the movie "The Godfather," 1975 (AP Photo).

Mafia Family (1985) was the basis for the film *Goodfellas* (1990) which I regard as one of the best organized crime movies extant. Joseph Pistone's *Donnie Brasco: My Undercover Life in the Mafia* (1987) relates how Pistone, an FBI undercover agent, infiltrated an LCN family for six years, gaining unprecedented access to the inner workings of the mob. *Donnie Brasco*, the subsequent film, starred Johnny Depp and Al Pacino.

Interestingly, Pacino also starred as Marlon Brando's (Don Corleone's) son and successor in *The Godfather* film series, as well as in the 1983 film *Scarface*, in which he played a Cuban drug lord, and *Carlito's Way* (1993), in which he plays a gangster, Carlito Brigante. Between them, Al Pacino and another Italian-American actor, Robert De Niro (*Analyze This, Analyze That, Goodfellas, Casino,* and *Raging Bull*), have made many film appearances either as Italian mobsters or as characters involved with the mob. As films, *Goodfellas* and *Donnie Brasco,* like *The Godfather,* expanded the audience from thousands of readers, to millions of viewers. Their potential impact therefore increased exponentially.

Other serious works of non-fiction by non-American authors have likewise targeted the mafia – in these cases in its original Italian, and specifically Sicilian, forms. To mention just a few, early works include books by Mori (1933), Hess (1973), Blok (1974), and Arlacchi (1986, et seq.), and more recently by Catanzaro (1992), Gambetta (1993), Stille (1995), Orlando (2001), and Paoli (2003). Hess, Blok and Gambetta focus on the mafia as an integral part of Sicilian life. Stille and Orlando describe the struggles and setbacks in attempting to combat its control of Sicilian society.

There have as well been a number of autobiographical and biographical accounts of life in organized crime. Any listing of them quickly establishes that they concentrate especially on LCN. Peter Maas's *The Valachi Papers* (1969) was made into a movie, as was Gay Talese's *Honor Thy Father* (1971). Vincent Teresa's *My Life in the Mafia* (1973), Jimmy "The Weasel" Fratianno's *The Last Mafioso,* as told to Ovid Demaris (1981), and Joseph Bonanno's *Man of Honor* (1983), are just a few examples of "tell-all" insider accounts of the mafia.

A review of the Mafia International website (http://glasgow-crew.tripod.com/mobbooks.html, accessed 4/13/06) for "mob books," listed fifty-five such offerings. The titles include *The Way of the Wiseguy, Cigar City Mafia, Blood and Honor, Takedown: The Fall of the Last Mafia Empire, Secrets of Life and Death: Women and the Mafia, Made Men,* and *Underboss: Sammy the Bull Gravano's Story of Life in the Mafia.* The continuing mafia concentration is quite evident.

References and further reading

By subject

American Mafia or *La Cosa Nostra*

Albini, J.L. *The American Mafia: genesis of a legend*. New York: Appleton-Century-Crofts, (Sociology Series), 1971

Anastasia, G. Blood and Honor: Inside the Scarfo Mob – The Mafia's Most Violent Family. New York: William Morrow, 1991

Anderson, A.G. *The Business of Organized Crime*. California: Stanford University Press (Hoover Institution), 1979

Bell, D. "Crime as an American way of life." *Antioch Reviews*, 13, Summer 1953

Bonanno, J. A Man of Honor: the Autobiography of Joseph Bonanno. New York: Simon & Schuster, 1983

Chambliss, W.J. *On the Take: From Petty Crooks to Presidents*. Bloomington & Indianapolis: Indiana University, published 1978; Second Edition 1988

Cressey, D.R. Theft of the Nation: The Structure and Operations of Organized Crime in America. New York: Harper and Row, 1969

Demaris, O. The Last Mafioso: the Treacherous World of Jimmy Fratianno. New York: Times Books, 1981

Firestone, T. "Mafia memoirs: What they tell us about organized crime." *Journal of Contemporary Criminal Justice*, 9(3), 1993

Fox, S. Blood and power: Organized crime in 20th century America. New York: William Morrow, 1989

Ianni, F.A.J. A Family Business: Kinship and Social Control in Organized Crime. Ithaca, New York: Russell Sage Foundation, 1972

Ianni, F.A.J., and E. Ruess-Ianni. "A Family Business: Business and Societal Organization in the Lupollo Family." In Ianni and Ruess-Ianni (eds.).

The Crime Society: Organized Crime and Corruption in America. New York: Times-Mirror, 1976

Maas, P. *The Valachi Papers.* New York: Bantam Books, 1969

New York Times. "Will the Real Mob Please Stand Up." March 5, 2006

Pileggi, N. *Wise Guy: Life in a Mafia Family.* New York: Simon & Schuster, 1985

Pistone, J. Donnie Brasco: My Undercover Life in the Mafia. New York: New Amer Library, 1987

Puzo, M., *The Godfather.* New York: GP Putnam's Sons, 1969

Raab, S. "Officials Say Mob Is Shifting Crimes To New Industries." *The New York Times*, February 10, 1997

Smith, D.C. *The Mafia Mystique.* New York: Basic Books, 1975

Talese, G. *Honor Thy Father.* New York: World Publishing, 1971

Teresa, V. *My Life in the Mafia.* Garden City, New York: Doubleday & Company, Inc, 1973

Businesses of organized crime

Clarke, R.V., and R. Brown. "International Trafficking in Stolen Vehicles." *Crime and Justice* 30, 2003

Eck, J.W., and J.G. Gersh. "Drug Trafficking as a Cottage Industry." In M. Natarajan and M. Hough (eds.). *Illegal Drug Markets: From Research to Prevention Policy*, Vol.11 of *Crime Prevention Studies*. Monsey, NY: Criminal Justice Press, 2000

Haller, M. "The changing structure of American gambling in the twentieth century." In E. Monkkonen (ed.). *Prostitution, drugs, gambling, and organized crime – Part 1.* New York: K. G. Saur, 1992

Jacobs, J.B. *Gotham Unbound.* New York: New York University Press, 1999

Lodhi, A., and E. Vaz. "Crime: A form of market transaction." *Canadian Journal of Criminology, 22(2), 1980*

Natarajan, M., and M. Belanger. "Varieties of Drug Trafficking Organizations: A Typology of Cases Prosecuted in New York City." *Journal of Drug Issues* 28, 1998

President's Initiative Against Illegal Logging. US Department of State Publication 11072, reference as sited in http://www.whitehouse.gov/infocus/illegal-logging/piail_brochure.pdf

Schelling, T.C. "What is the Business of Organized Crime?" *Journal of Public Law* 20, 1971

Secretary-General's Report. *Prevention of crimes that infringe on the cultural heritage of peoples in the form of movable property.* Commission on Crime Prevention and Criminal Justice, Thirteenth Session, Vienna 2004, E/CN.15/2004/1

Von Lampe, K. "The trafficking in untaxed cigarettes in Germany: A case study of the social embeddedness of illegal markets." In P.C. von Duyne, K. von Lampe, N. Passas (eds.). *Upperworld and Underworld in Cross-Border Crime.* Nijmegen: Wolf Legal Publishers, 2002

Chinese Mafia

Bingsong, H. "Organized Crime: A Perspective from China." In J.S. Albanese, D.K. Das, and A. Verma (eds.). *Organized Crime: World Perspectives,* Upper Saddle River, NJ: Prentice Hall, 2003

Chin, K. Heijin: Organized Crime, Business, and Politics in Taiwan. Armonk, NY: M.E. Sharpe, 2003

—— Smuggled Chinese: Clandestine Immigration into the United States. Philadelphia: Temple University Press, 1999

—— "Transnational Organized Crime Activities." Paper presented at International Scientific and Professional Advisory Council conference in Courmayer, Italy, 25–27 September 1998. Available: School of Criminal Justice, Rutgers University

—— Chinese Triad Societies, Tongs, Organized Crime, and Street Gangs in Asia and the United States. Ph.D. dissertation, University of Pennsylvania, 1986

Chu, Y.K. "Hong Kong Triads after 1997. *Trends in Organized Crime,* 8:3, Spring 2005

—— *The Triads as Business.* London and New York: Routledge, 2000

Finckenauer, J.O., and K. Chin. "Asian Transnational Organized Crime and its Impact on the United States: Developing a Transnational Crime Research Agenda." A final report for the National Institute of Justice. November 2004 (http://www.ncjrs.gov/pdffiles1/nij/grants/213310.pdf)

Lo, T.W. *Corruption and Politics in Hong Kong and China.* Buckingham: Open University Press, 1993

Posner, G.L. Warlords of crime: Chinese secret societies – the new Mafia. New York: McGraw-Hill, 1988

Combating organized crime

Beare, M.E., and F.T. Martens. "Policing Organized Crime: The Comparative Structures, Traditions and Policies Within the United States and Canada." *Journal of Contemporary Criminal Justice* 14:4. November 1998

Jacobs, J.B. *Mobsters, Unions, and Feds.* New York: New York University Press, 2006

Kendall, R.E. "Responding to transnational crime." *Transnational Organized Crime* 4:3 &4, 1998

Layne, M., S. Decker, M. Townsend, and C. Chester. "Measuring the Deterrent Effect of Enforcement Operations on Drug Smuggling, 1991–1999." *Trends in Organized Crime*, 7:3, Spring 2002

Maltz, M. *Measuring the Effectiveness of Organized Crime Control Efforts.* Chicago: Office of International Criminal Justice. University of Illinois at Chicago, 1990

General

Adamoli, S., A. Di Nicola, W.U. Savona, and P. Zoffi. *Organised Crime Around the World.* Helsinki, Finland: Heuni, 1998

Albanese, J. *Organized Crime in America.* 3rd ed. Cincinnati: Anderson Publishing, 1996

English, T.J. *Paddy Whacked.* New York: HarperCollins, 2005

Keene, L.L. "Asian Organized Crime." *FBI Law Enforcement Bulletin*, 58, October 1989

Kelly, R. *Organized Crime: A Global Perspective.* Rowman and Littlefield, 1986

Kenney, D.J., and J.O. Finckenauer. *Organized Crime in America.* Belmont, CA: Wadsworth Publishing Company, 1995

Pennsylvania Crime Commission. 1991 Report. St. Davids, PA., 1991

Potter, G.W. Criminal Organizations: Vice, Racketeering, and Politics in an American City. Long Grove, IL: Waveland Press, Inc., 1994

President's Commission on Organized Crime. "The Impact: Organized Crime Today." Washington, DC: Government Printing Office, 1986

Ryan, P.J. *Organized Crime: A reference Handbook.* Santa Barbara, CA: ABC-CLIO, Inc., 1995

Trends in Organized Crime, 5:4, Summer 2000

United Nations Centre for International Crime Prevention (UN CICP). Global Studies on Organized Crime. "Transnational Organized Crime: Dangerousness and Trends." September 2000

—— "Assessing Transnational Organized Crime: Results of a Pilot Survey of 40 Selected Organized Criminal Groups in 16 Countries." *Trends in Organized Crime* 6:2, Winter 2000

United Nations Convention Against Transnational Organized Crime. Excerpt in *Trends in Organized Crime* 5:4, Summer 2000

United Nations Convention on Transnational Organized Crime. 2000 http://untreaty.un.org/English/notpubl/18–12E.doc

United Nations Office for Drug Control and Crime Prevention. *Global Report on Crime and Justice.* New York and Oxford: Oxford University Press, 1999

United Nations Office on Drugs and Crime. *Trends in Crime and Justice*, March 2005, unpublished

van Dijk, J.J.M. "The experience of crime and justice" *Global Report on Crime and Justice.* New York and Oxford: Oxford University Press, 1999

Human trafficking

Andreas, P. *Border Games: Policing: Policing the US-Mexico Divide.* Ithaca, NY: Cornell University Press, 2001

Brazil, D. No Money, No Honey!: A Candid Look at Sex-for-Sale in Singapore. Singapore: Angsana Books, 2004

Denisova, T.A. "Trafficking in Women and Children for Purposes of Sexual Exploitation: The Criminological Aspect." In J.O. Finckenauer and J.L. Schrock (eds.). *The Prediction and Control of Organized Crime.* New Brunswick, USA: Transaction Publishers, 2004

Emerton, R. "Trafficking of women into Hong Kong for the purpose of prostitution: Preliminary research findings." Occasional Paper No. 3. Hong Kong: University of Hong Kong, 2001

Estes, R.J., and N.A. Weiner. "Child Sexual Exploitation in Canada, Mexico and the US" A report of the United States National Study. "The Commercial Sexual Exploitation of Children in the US, Canada and Mexico," 2001 (http://caster.ssw.upenn.edu/~restes/CSEC_Files/Complete_CSEC_020220.pdf)

Finckenauer, J.O., and J. Schrock. "Human Trafficking: A Growing Criminal Market in the US" Publication for the International Center, National Institute of Justice http://www.ojp.usdoj.gov/nij/international/ht.html)

Gittelsohn, J. "US Sends Strong Message to Those Who Traffic in Human Lives US" Department of State Electronic Journals. June 1, 2003 http://usinfo.state.gov/journals/itgic/0603/ijge/gj04.htm

Global Patterns. April 2006 http://www.unodc.org/pdf/traffickinginpersons_report_2006ver2.pdf

Hughes, D.M., and T.A. Denisova. "The Transnational Political Criminal Nexus of Trafficking in Women from Ukraine." In J.O. Finckenauer and J.L. Schrock (eds.). *The Prediction and Control of Organized Crime.* New Brunswick, USA: Transaction Publishers, 2004

Kwong, P. Forbidden Workers: illegal Chinese Immigrants and American Labor. New York: New Press, 1997

Kyle, D. "Profiting from Disparity and Desperation." A briefing for "wideangle," WNET New York, Thirteen, September 22, 2003 (www.pbs.org/wnet/wideangle/shows/dying/index.html)

Kyle, D., and R. Koslowski (eds.). *Global Human Smuggling.* Baltimore & London: The Johns Hopkins University Press, 2001

Landesman, P. "The Girls Next Door." *The New York Times.* January 25, 2004

Liang, Z., and Wenzhen Y. "From Fujian to New York: Understanding the New Chinese Immigration." In David Kyle and Rey Koslowski (eds.). *Global Human Smuggling.* Baltimore & London: The Johns Hopkins University Press, 2001

O'Neill Richard, A. "International Trafficking in Women to United States: A Contemporary Manifestation of Slavery and Organized Crime." DCI Exceptional Intelligence Analyst Program. Washington, D.C.: Center for the Study of Intelligence, 1999

Raymond, J., and D. Hughes. *Sex Trafficking of Women in the United States: International and Domestic Trends.* North Amhearst, MA: Coalition Against Trafficking in Women, 2001

Smith, P.J. (ed.). Human Smuggling: Chinese Migrant Trafficking and the Challenge to America's Immigration Tradition. Washington, D.C.: Center for Strategic and International Studies, 1997

United Nations Office on Drugs and Crime. *Trafficking in Persons Protocol.* Convention Against Transnational Organized Crime, Vienna, 2000

—— Trafficking in Persons: Global Patterns, Vienna, 2006

Italian and Sicilian Mafia

Arlacchi, P. Mafia Business: the Mafia Ethic and the Spirit of Capitalism. Oxford: Oxford University Press, 1986

Blok, A. The Mafia of a Sicilian Village 1860–1960: a Study of Violent Peasant Entrepreneurs. Oxford: Basil Blackwell, 1974

Catanzaro, R. Men of Respect: a Social History of the Sicilian Mafia. Old Tappan, New Jersey: Free Press, 1992

di Argentine, A.B. "The Mafias in Italy." In Ernesto U. Savona (ed.). Mafia Issues: Analyses and proposals for combating the mafia today. International Scientific and Professional Advisory Council of the United Nationals Crime and Prevention and Criminal Justice Programme (ISPAC), 1992

Dickie, J. Cosa Nostra: a History of the Sicilian Mafia. London: Palgrave Macmillan, 2004

Gambetta, D. The Sicilian Mafia: the Business of Private Protection. Cambridge, Mass.: Harvard University Press, 1993

Hess, H. Mafia & Mafiosi: the Structure of Power. London: Saxon House, 1973

Mori, C. The Last Struggle With the Mafia. London: Putnam, 1933

Orlando, L. Fighting the Mafia and Renewing Sicilian Culture. San Francisco: Encounter Books, 2001

Paoli, L. "Italian Organised Crime: Mafia Associations and Criminal Enterprises." Global Crime, 6:1, February 2004

—— Mafia Brotherhoods: Organized Crime, Italian Style. New York: Oxford University Press Inc., 2003

Schneider, J.C., and P.T. Schneider. Reversible Destiny: Mafia, Antimafia, and the Struggle for Palermo. University of California Press, 2003

Stille, A. Excellent Cadavers: the Mafia and the Death of the First Italian Republic. New York: Pantheon Press, 1995

Tilly, C. Foreword to Anton Blok, The Mafia of a Sicilian Village. Oxford: Basil Blackwell, 1974

Vitale, P. "Dining with a Godfather." Trends in Organized Crime, 9:1, 2005

Japanese *Yakuza*

Hill, P. "The Changing Face of the Yakuza." In M. Galeotti (ed.). Global Crime Today. Abingdon: Routledge, 2005

Kaplan, D.E., and A. Dubro. *Yakuza: The Explosive Account of Japan's Criminal Underworld*. Reading, MA: Addison-Wesley, 1986

Uchiyama, A. "Organized Crime: A Perspective from Japan." In J. Albanese, D. Das, and A. Verma (eds.). *Organized Crime: World Perspectives*. Upper Saddle River, NJ: Prentice-Hall, 2003

Media and organized crime

Cohen, R. "Mob succumbs to movie magic." *The Washington Post*, April 13, 2006

Cohen, S. Folk Devils and Moral Panics: The Creation of the Mods and Rockers. Oxford: Basil Blackwell, 1990

Dika, V. "The Representation of Ethnicity in *The Godfather*." In F.F. Coppola's *The Godfather Trilogy*, ed. N. Browner, Cambridge: Cambridge University Press, 2000

Haberman, C. "As 'Sopranos' Returns, Art Irritates Life." *NY Times*. March 10, 2006

Larke, G.S. "Organized crime: Mafia myths in film and television." In Paul Mason (ed.). *Criminal Visions: Media representations of crime and justice*. Devon, UK: Willan Publishing, 2003

Other

Barker, T. "One Percent Bikers Clubs: A Description." *Trends in Organized Crime*, 9:1, Fall 2005

BBC Monitoring International Reports. November 22, 2003

Bruneau, T.C. *Strategic Insights*. Volume IV, Issue 5, May 2005

Conseil de l'Europa. Comité d'experts sur les aspects de droit penal et las aspects criminologiques de la criminalité (PC-CO). Questionnaire: Strasbourg, France, August 1997

Glaser, C. *Bo Tsotsi: the Youth Gangs of Soweto, 1935–1976*. Westport, CT: Greenwood Press, 2000

Healy, P. "Investigators Say Fraud Ring Staged Thousands of Crashes." *New York Times*. August 12, 2003

Johnson, S., and D.B. Muhlhausen. "North American Transnational Youth Gangs: Breaking the Chain of Violence." *Trends in Organized Crime*, 9:1, Fall 2005

Park, Y.K. "Transnational organized crime and the countermeasures in Korea." In UNAFEI, *Resource material series* No. 58. Tokyo, Japan: Asia and Far East Institute for the Prevention of Crime and the Treatment of Offenders (UNAFEI), Dec., 2001

Schatzberg, R., and R.J. Kelly. *African American Organized Crime: A Social History*. New Brunswick, NJ: Rutgers University Press, 1997

Russian Mafia

Finckenauer, J.O., and E.J. Waring. *Russian Mafia in America: Immigration, Culture, and Crime*. Boston: Northeastern University Press, 1998

Varese, F. *The Russian Mafia*. Oxford: Oxford University Press, 2001.

Volkov, V. Violent Entrepreneurs: The Use of Force in the making of Russian Capitalism. Ithaca: Cornell University Press, 2002

Theory and explanation

Albanese, J. "The Prediction and Control of Organized Crime: A Risk Assessment Instrument for Targeting Law Enforcement Efforts." In J.O. Finckenauer and J.L. Schrock (eds.). *The Prediction and Control of Organized Crime*. New Brunswick, USA: Transaction Publishers, 2004

—— "The Causes of Organized Crime: Do Criminals Organize Around Opportunities for Crime or Do Criminal Opportunities Create New Offenders?" *Contemporary Criminal Justice* 16, November 2000

Albini, J.L. "Donald Cressey's contributions to the study of organized crime: An evaluation." *Crime and Delinquency* 34(3), 1988

Cloward, R.A., and L.E. Ohlin. *Delinquency and Opportunity: A Theory of Delinquent Gangs*. New York: Free Press, 1960

Cohen, L.E., and M. Felson. "Social Change and Crime Rate Trends: A Routine Activity Approach." American Sociological Review 44, 1979

Cornish, D., and R.V. Clarke (eds.). *The Reasoning Criminal: Rational Choice Perspectives on Offending*. New York, NY: Springer –Verlag, 1986

"Countering Crime and Corruption: Furthering a Culture of Lawfulness." *Trends in Organized Crime*, 4:2, Winter 1998

Cressey, D.R. "Organized crime and inner city youth." *Crime and Delinquency*, April 1970

Hagan, F.E. "The Organized Crime Continuum: A Further Specification of a New Conceptual Model." *Criminal Justice Review* 8, 1983

Ianni, F.A.J. *Black Mafia; Ethnic Succession in Organized Crime.* New York: Simon and Schuster, 1974

Lupsha, P. "Individual choice, materials culture, and organized crime." *Criminology*, 18, 1981

Maltz, M. "Defining Organized Crime." In R.J. Kelly, K. Chin, and R. Schatzberg (eds.). *Handbook of Organized Crime in the United States.* Westport, Conn. and London: Greenwood Press, 1994

—— "Toward Defining Orgainzed Crime." In H.E. Alexander and G. Caiden (eds.). *The Politics and Economics of Organized Crime.* Lexington, MA: D.C. Heath, 1985

Miller, W.B. "Lower class culture as a generating milieu of gang delinquency." *Journal of Social Issues*, 14(3), 1958

National Research Council. *Transnational Organized Crime: Summary of a Workshop.* Washington, DC: National Academy Press, 1999

Naylor, R.T. "Mafias, Myths and Markets: On the Theory and Practice of Enterprise Crime." *Transnational Organized Crime*, 3:3, 1997

O'Kane, J. The Crooked Ladder: Gangster Ethnicity and the American Dream. New Brunswick, NJ: Transaction, 1992

Reuter, P. "Research on American Organized Crime." In R.B. Kelly, K. Chin, and R. Schatzberg (eds.). *Handbook of Organized Crime in the United States.* Westport, Connecticut: Greenwood Press, 1994

Schrag, C. *Crime and justice: American style.* Rockville, MD: National Institute of Mental Health, Center for Study of Crime and Delinquency, 1971

Sellin, T. *Culture Conflict and Crime.* New York: Social Science Research Counsel, 1938

Shaw, C.R., and H.D. McKay. *Juvenile Delinquency and Urban Areas.* Chicago: University of Chicago Press, 1942

Smith, D.C. "Paragons, pariahs, and pirates: A spectrum-based theory of enterprise." *Crime and Delinquency*, 26, 1980

Thrasher, F. M. *The gang.* Chicago, IL: University of Chicago Press, 1927

van Dijk, J.J.M., and K. Kangaspunta. "Piecing Together the Cross-National Crime Puzzle." *National Institute of Justice Journal*, January 2000

— "Does Crime Pay? On the Relationship between Crime, Rule of Law and Economic Growth." *Forum on Crime and Society*, 1:1, 2001

Index

Note: Page references in *italics* indicate illustrations; those in **bold type** indicate text boxes.